Neighborhood Upgrading

SUNY Series in Urban Public Policy

Mark Schneider and Richard Rich, Editors

Neighborhood Upgrading

A Realistic Assessment

David P. Varady

State University of New York Press

Published by
State University of New York Press, Albany

©1986 State University of New York

All rights reserved

Printed in the United States of America

No part of this book may be used or reproduced
in any manner whatsoever without written permission
except in the case of brief quotations embodied in
critical articles and reviews.

For information, address State University of New York
Press, State University Plaza, Albany, N.Y., 12246

Library of Congress Cataloging in Publication Data

Varady, David P.
  Neighborhood upgrading.

  (SUNY series on urban public policy)
  Bibliography: p. 165
  Includes index.
    1. Urban renewal—United States. 2. Urban home-
steading—United States. 3. Urban policy—United
States. 4. Neighborhood—United States. 5. Community
development, Urban—United States. I. Title. II. Series.
HT175.V37   1986   307.3'362'0973   85-30392
ISBN 0-88706-299-7
ISBN 0-88706-300-4 (pbk.)

Contents

Figures

Tables

Acknowledgments

Gratitude is expressed to the U.S. Department of Housing and Urban Development for making available the Urban Homesteading Demonstration data sets on which much of this book is based.

This book would not have been possible without the assistance of many people. In particular, I want to thank Larry Hodes (HUD) for his insights into neighborhood revitalization programs, including urban homesteading, and Carla Pedone (formerly of Urban Systems Research and Engineering Inc.) for patiently explaining the intricacies of the Urban Homesteading Demonstration data sets.

I also want to express my appreciation to Dennis Gale (George Washington University), George Galster (Wooster College), Stephen Golant (University of Florida), Samuel Klausner (University of Pennsylvania), Gregory Lipton (University of Virginia) and Howard Sumka (HUD) for their comments as well as expertise.

Most of all, I want to thank my wife Adrienne for editing the manuscript and for her emotional support.

Several of the chapters have appeared previously in different form in professional journals: Chapter 1 in *The Journal of Planning Literature*, Chapter 3 in *Regional Science Perspectives*, Chapter 6 in *The Journal of the American Planning Association*, and Chapter 8 in *The Journal of Architectural and Planning Research*.

Introduction

The image of America's urban neighborhoods has changed drastically over the past forty years. Between the end of World War II and the mid-1970s, the picture was gloomy. Newspaper stories and television programs highlighted the massive destruction and devastation of inner-city neighborhoods citing widespread patterns of housing abandonment. The South Bronx was perhaps the most infamous example of this problem. President Carter visited the area on October 5, 1977 and promised massive doses of federal funds. Ecological and economic theories also supported the gloomy outlook. Neighborhood change was viewed as an inevitable evolutionary process of deterioration, and, since decline was viewed as inevitable, the only appropriate role for government was to plan for the reuse of the land.

Since the mid-1970s, a more upbeat image has emerged. Hundreds of neighborhoods in cities throughout the United States have experienced gentrification, the replacement of a working-class or lower class population by a middle-class one. Young professional couples are attracted to these neighborhoods by the historically distinctive architecture and by their proximity to central business districts. By now, the subject of gentrification has been well researched (Gale, 1984).

There is increasing interest in a second type of revitalization, "incumbent upgrading" (Clay, 1979), where improvements in housing and social conditions occur as the result of the efforts of existing residents, and where the existing population (or the same type of population) remains in place. The War on Poverty and later the Model Cities program provided the impetus for self-help

1

efforts in poor sections of the city, often with large minority populations. Such indigenous improvement efforts spread to white ethnic areas in the late 1970s.

Gentrified and upgraded areas differ. The latter tend to have less distinctive housing and are located further from central business districts. Government plays a far more substantial role in upgrading areas through such programs as the Neighborhood Housing Service, Urban Homesteading (both of which will be described in greater detail below), and the Community Development Block Grant Program (CDBG).

Research on neighborhood upgrading is at a primitive stage. One problem is the exaggerated focus on improvements in housing conditions and other physical characteristics of the neighborhood. Myers and Binder (1977; p. 6) use the umbrella of conservation to refer to "all these efforts that are aimed at stabilizing or renewing a city's housing and commercial stock." Clay (1979; p. 7) indicates that the main feature of incumbent upgrading is *physical improvement* by existing residents. These definitions are too narrow because they exclude situations where the socioeconomic level of the population is declining and where it may be necessary to slow or stop these declines in order to successfully implement any housing rehabilitation programs. Our criticism of the definition of upgrading is more than semantic. Much of the CDBG funds has gone to areas experiencing socioeconomic decline. As a result of the overly narrow definition of upgrading, most of the research fails to address the prospects for upgrading in these declining areas.

Further, most of the available research is impressionistic, relying on mailed questionnaires or interviews with city officials and private community leaders. Statistical evidence on the *existence of improvements* is virtually nonexistent, and, consequently, virtually nothing is known about the incidence of *successful* incumbent upgrading other than in already stable white ethnic communities.

There are numerous examples in the literature (discussed in greater detail in the next chapter) of unsupported claims about the value of different governmental neighborhood preservation programs. This is certainly illustrated by the exaggerated claims made about the Neighborhood Housing Services program (see, for example Clay, 1979) but is also shown by claims about other programs like Urban Homesteading.

The problem with these assertions is that policymakers have often accepted them as facts. They have gleaned the more optimistic assertions from the Clay and Myers studies and used them as a basis for policymaking. Later chapters will show that there is little factual basis for this optimism.

More generally, this book takes a hard realistic look at government housing rehabilitation programs and the role that they can play in neighborhood upgrading efforts through research on the federal government's Urban Homesteading Demonstration (UHD). Under this program, vacant properties owned by the government are sold to families for a dollar, providing the families agree to live in them for at least three years and bring them up to code standards. it is assumed that the existence of homesteading activity would raise confidence levels among existing neighboring residents, causing them to remain at their locations and improve their own properties. It is also assumed that the homesteading activity would attract middle-income families, who might not otherwise consider living in these areas.

The book has four more specific purposes. First, it synthesizes what is known about neighborhood change to identify where it is feasible to intervene in the neighborhood decline process (Chapter 1). We examine all of the causes of neighborhood decline including one—racial succession—that is controversial. In the past, social scientists, like middle-class Americans in general, have been reluctant to discuss race related issues, fearing that they would be considered racist. At the risk of being labeled discriminatory, I will discuss the link between race and neighborhood decline, believing that a frank exploration of this subject is the only way to begin to develop effective realistic solutions. Later chapters will show that income shifts associated with racial change, rather than racial shifts per se, are a key cause of neighborhood decline. This book advocates that policymakers and social scientists stop sidestepping the role of population shifts in explaining neighborhood change.

Second, the study measures the neighborhood impacts of the UHD program. How did the UHD neighborhoods fare, relative to their cities and to control neighborhoods in these cities during the 1970 to 1980 period (Chapter 3)? In addition, through a case study of one UHD neighborhood, the Wynnefield community in Philadelphia, we highlight the difficulties of achieving upgrading in a racially changing community (Chapter 4).

Third, the book assesses the impact of the UHD on the attitudes and behavior of nonhomesteading families in these areas. What impact did the program have on confidence levels (Chapter 5)? What was the relative importance of the program, as compared to other background characteristics, in explaining variations in the likelihood of moving (Chapter 6) or in making property investments (Chapter 7)? To what extent are fears concerning the negative impacts of rehabilitation activity on the elderly supported (Chapter 8)? That is, did such rehabilitation lead to sharply rising housing costs and shattered social patterns?

Finally, we draw from the empirical results to identify those communities where programs like Urban Homesteading are most likely to support upgrading efforts. Where Urban Homesteading is shown to have potential, the book indicates what ancillary government services (such as technical assistance to neighborhood organizations) may be helpful in these improvement efforts. Where the prospects for success through such localistic programs are poor, we discuss the broader metropolitan-wide social and economic policies that are necessary to stabilize both the population and the housing stock.

The significance of this study extends beyond the Urban Homesteading Demonstration program. With the increased flexibility possible under the CDBG program, many local planners are using upgrading strategies similar to that used in the Demonstration (i.e., housing rehabilitation combined with public improvements implemented in areas at the beginning of the decline process). The distinctive feature of homesteading is the highly visible rehabilitation. If we are unable to detect any indirect neighborhood effects in this study, it is highly unlikely that these effects would occur in areas with the more standard forms of rehabilitation.

Chapter *1*

Neighborhood Upgrading: A Literature Review

Since the end of World War II, federal housing policy has shifted from new construction and slum clearance to housing rehabilitation and neighborhood upgrading.[1] With the implementation of the Community Development Block Grant Legislation in 1975, housing rehabilitation has become the dominant local activity (Sacco, 1984). Despite the great expansion in neighborhood upgrading programs, relatively little attention has been given to the feasibility of these efforts to slow or stop physical and social decline with the existing population remaining in place. This chapter synthesizes what is known about the types of programs most likely to be successful in particular types of communities. The first part of this chapter reviews the theoretical literature on neighborhood decline and improvement. The second examines recent writings on neighborhood upgrading, while the last reviews existing empirical studies on the "spillover" effects of government funded housing programs.

Theories of Neighborhood Change

A. Three perspectives on neighborhood decline and improvement

Effective neighborhood stabilization programs require sound theories of the causes of neighborhood decline and improvement.

In a seminal 1982 article, Solomon and Vandell review the three major theories of decline.

1. ORTHODOX ECONOMIC THEORY. This theory assumes complete economic rationality among all the actors in the housing market. Landlords and owners seek to maximize the utility they derive from their properties subject to budget constraints. Neighborhood decline results from the softening of demand for housing in local markets and the impact that this has on cash flows. The softening of demand may result from "pulls," positive factors external to the market. An example is the construction of modern homes on the fringe of the metropolitan area which draws middle-income families away from the central city. On the other hand, the weakening of demand often reflects "pushes," negative factors internal to the neighborhood. For example, the inmigration of low-income families of a different racial group may cause existing families to "panic move."[2]

The outmigration of upwardly mobile families from central city neighborhoods initiates a process whereby the housing declines in value and is occupied by members of successively lower income groups. This process, commonly referred to as "filtering," is viewed as desirable according to this theory because housing opportunities are made available to lower income families.

Once the process of decline begins, it develops a momentum of its own. Landlords perceiving (or anticipating) the inmigration of lower income families with a decreased ability to afford rental payments may withhold needed repairs. Similarly, owner occupants may forgo property improvements if they assume that income shifts will reduce property values. Poorer maintenance decreases the likelihood of middle-income families moving into the area, thus speeding the process of decline. It is usually assumed that once the process begins, neighborhoods go through clearcut stages of deterioration leading ultimately to widespread abandonment (Birch, 1971, cited in Kolodny, 1983).

The main weakness of the theory is the lack of specificity regarding the main cause(s) of decline. Does housing obsolescence cause income change or does income change lead to declines in housing quality? Many economists argue that the aging of dwelling units is the prime cause of neighborhood physical and social decline. That is, over time, buildings necessarily deteriorate due to obsolescence and wear and tear; and this deterioration facilitates the filtering of the housing to lower income families (Muth, 1975, p. 68; Quigley, 1979, p. 417). This explanation of decline suggests the need for housing maintenance and repair programs to prevent neighborhood physical and social deterioration.

2. DUAL THEORY. Key actors in certain neighborhood housing markets do not emphasize economic rationality but, rather, reciprocal personal relationships. Landlords may charge lower than market rents, and, in return, tenants may assume many of the responsibilities for repairs. Similarly, homeowners do not necessarily seek the highest prices for their homes. A strong sense of loyalty to neighbors may cause them to avoid working through realtors, who might bring in "outsiders." Instead, such homeowners rely on informal contacts to find interested buyers. Dual markets typically occur in homogeneous white ethnic communities.

The basic cause of decline in dual markets is a breakdown in the reciprocity relationship. This may be due to a weakening of demand. For example, children raised in the community may not be interested in living there, or landlords may be forced to take in "outsiders" as tenants. Decreased homogeneity leads to a weakening of social bonds, and the foundation for this type of market disappears.

The theory provides ambiguous policy implications. That is, it supports efforts to maintain homogeneous ethnic communities, whereas most local governments are committed to heterogeneity at the neighborhood level.

3. RADICAL THEORY. These writers focus on disparities in power between the different actors in neighborhood housing markets (e.g., tenants versus landlords, homeowners versus banks). Private and public institutions are seen as the "culprits" in neighborhood decline through "blockbusting" (realtor-induced panic selling), "redlining" (the withholding of mortgage and improvement loans from racially mixed areas), poorly designed housing subsidy programs, and the like. These theorists emphasize the need to reduce power imbalances through neighborhood self-help and by transferring real estate to

neighborhood residents, as is done with community development corporations.

B. Recent theoretical writings

1. INCOME AND RACIAL SHIFTS AS CAUSES OF NEIGHBORHOOD DECLINE. Grigsby, Baratz, and Maclennan (1984, p. 46) criticize the widely accepted belief that the aging of the housing stock is the primary cause of neighborhood decline.

Figure 1.1. **How social and economic changes alter characteristics of housing inventory and neighborhoods** (Read clockwise from Panel A)

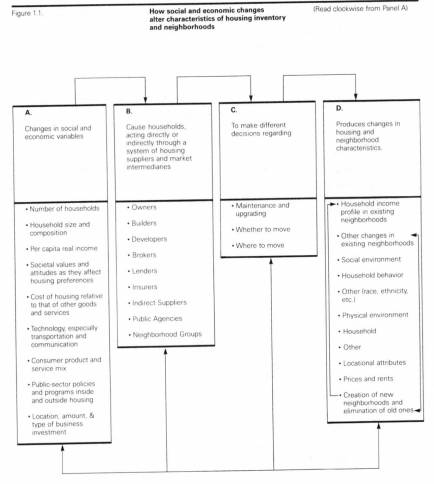

A.	B.	C.	D.
Changes in social and economic variables	Cause households, acting directly or indirectly through a system of housing suppliers and market intermediaries	To make different decisions regarding	Produces changes in housing and neighborhood characteristics.

• Number of households	• Owners	• Maintenance and upgrading	• Household income profile in existing neighborhoods
• Household size and composition	• Builders	• Whether to move	• Other changes in existing neighborhoods
• Per capita real income	• Developers	• Where to move	
	• Brokers		• Social environment
• Societal values and attitudes as they affect housing preferences	• Lenders		• Household behavior
	• Insurers		• Other (race, ethnicity, etc.)
• Cost of housing relative to that of other goods and services	• Indirect Suppliers		• Physical environment
	• Public Agencies		• Household
• Technology, especially transportation and communication	• Neighborhood Groups		• Other
			• Locational attributes
• Consumer product and service mix			• Prices and rents
• Public-sector policies and programs inside and outside housing			• Creation of new neighborhoods and elimination of old ones
• Location, amount, & type of business investment			

Source: Grigsby et. al., 1984:33

> The quickness with which the forces of nature move in when
> man is no longer interested in resisting them is readily perceived
> in neighborhoods that are in the path of a highway development
> or part of an urban redevelopment site. But man is the key, not
> nature.

Physical deterioration is a *consequence* rather than a *cause* of
population succession (Figure 1.1). Changes in social and
economic variables at the societal, metropolitan or city level cause
homeowners to reduce spending on improvements or to move
away. (An example of a "social change" is an urban renewal project which results in the displacement of low-income families to adjoining communities, thereby initiating social and physical decline
in the latter areas.) The aggregation of numerous individual
household (and landlord) decisions produces changes in
neighborhood population and housing characteristics which, in
turn, affect the moving and repair decisions of other residents
and prospective residents.

Neighborhood income changes alone do not explain the rapid
physical and social deterioration of many central city
neighborhoods. The behavioral characteristics of *some* low-
income families (vandalism, theft, poor housekeeping) "produce
high operating costs for landlords and extra expenses for the
public sector adding to the amount of decline that would be expected from low income alone" (Grigsby, Baratz and Maclennan,
1984, p. 55). Furthermore, the spatial concentration of low-
income families exacerbates the problems of poverty by contributing to a sense of alienation and hopelessness, thereby reducing the possibilities for social mobility (Downs, 1981). Presumably,
such concentrations lead to more rapid physical deterioration
than would occur if this low-income population were dispersed
throughout the metropolitan area.

It is impossible to overlook racial change as an element in
neighborhood succession and decline, particularly in eastern and
midwestern cities, since so much (but certainly not all) of the
decline has occurred in the path of expanding black ghettos.
Although there is a relatively large body of research on
neighborhood racial change (Goering, 1978) and on ghetto expansion patterns (Rose, 1971), there has been minimal linkage be-

tween these subjects and theoretical works on neighborhood physical and social decline.

In fact, the tendency for ghetto expansion to lead to neighborhood decline is attributable to income rather than racial change. At first, racial transition involves little or no socioeconomic change. The first black inmigrants typically have income and educational levels equal to or higher than existing white residents (Aldrich, 1975; Taeuber and Taeuber, 1965). However, these middle income blacks are usually unsuccessful in separating themselves spatially from lower-income black families. Racial succession is followed by income succession as the initial black residents move further from the center of the city. *It is the replacement of middle by lower class black families that explains much of the decline associated with ghetto growth.*

However, it is a mistake to completely overlook the racial dimension of neighborhood decline.[3] Distrust between white landlords and black tenants often causes the former to forgo needed repairs and the latter to take an overly casual attitude toward apartment upkeep (Sternlieb, 1966). Furthermore, the rapid population turnover resulting from white panic moving undercuts the neighborhood social fabric through the closing of churches, synagogues and other institutions, thereby decreasing the feasibility of self-help efforts.

Leven, et al. (1976) used an arbitrage model to explain the relation between black ghetto expansion and housing decline, and theirs is one of the few studies to examine neighborhood decline in the context of ghetto expansion patterns.

Whites in St. Louis, as elsewhere, lived in mostly white areas closer to the suburbs, while blacks lived in a segregated zone closer to the urban center. A transition zone separated the two areas. Housing values in St. Louis dropped in anticipation of racial change, as the boundary of the black ghetto shifted toward the white community. The declines in prices reflected the withdrawal of white housing demand from these areas. These drops in prices provided housing opportunities for middle-income black families, while simultaneously leading to a temporary rise in prices. After middle income black demand was satisfied, lower income blacks succeeded in moving into the area, with lower income levels and accompanying drops in prices.

A parallel shift occurred in the rental market. Landlords were forced to adjust to the decreased attractiveness of the area to middle-income families by reducing rents. With the lower rents, landlords were unable to afford adequate maintenance. With decreased repairs, the condition of the rental stock deteriorated rapidly.

Social class changes accompanying racial transition often contribute to an even more serious problem than price declines: an increase in violent street crime (see, for example, Y. Ginsberg, 1975; Molotch, 1972; and Wilkes, 1971).[4] Two additional factors besides social class changes contribute to the security problem. First, racial change typically involves the replacement of an aging white population by a younger black one; and teenagers and young adults are more prone toward criminality than those in older age cohorts. Second, racially changing areas often attract restless low-income youths from inner-city ghetto communities who commit much of the crime (Molotch, 1972).

Neighborhoods like The Ville in St. Louis are the culmination of racial and social class shifts (Schoenberg and Rosenbaum, 1980). This was originally the cultural heart of black St. Louis. The outmigration of middle-class blacks to the suburbs led to income declines and high rate of population turnover. More importantly, the lack of a stable middle- or working-class population contributed to a lack of surveillance over strangers and a high incidence of crime.

The preceding explanation of neighborhood decline suggests the need for both metropolitan policies as well as programs implemented within these areas. The former would address the underlying causes of decline: poverty, income, and racial segregation. The latter would focus either on stabilizing racially mixed middle-class areas (thereby forestalling income succession), or, conceding the inevitability of racial succession, on attempting to preserve predominantly middle-class black areas. The research literature provides little basis for optimism about either localistic strategy.

The stereotype—that once racial change begins, complete or almost complete turnover occurs—is supported by reality.[5] There are very few examples of successful stabilization efforts in racially mixed communities adjacent to black ghetto areas. Most of the handful of success stories are in communities where large institutions have played a key role in promoting stabilization (e.g., the University of Chicago in the Hyde Park-Kenwood section of that city).

Stabilization efforts have usually failed because they have ignored the pressure of black housing demand on the community which is the underlying cause of racial turnover (Aldrich, 1975). The typical approach in white middle-class communities has been to work through the local resident association to achieve stability. These efforts have been hampered by the reluctance of resident association leaders to even discuss the issues of race and racial change, let alone formulate programs to deal with these issues. Many middle-class whites fear that they will be considered racist if they discuss racial issues (Molotch, 1972; Wireman, 1984).

Resident associations have instead attempted to maintain the overall quality of life, assuming that this would indirectly lead to racial stabilization. Typical association activities include running street fairs, publishing community newspapers, organizing block clubs, lobbying for better public services and facilities, and working on the community master plan. These efforts rarely stop or even slow down racial change. In fact, they may even accelerate the process by making an area more attractive to home-seeking blacks. At the same time, these efforts have little or no impact on home-seeking whites, who have many more options available to them and typically avoid areas where racial change is an issue.

In recent years, as the boundary of the black ghetto has extended past the limits of the central city of many American metropolitan areas, racial change has become a suburban, as well as a central city, phenomenon. Most of the innovative localistic programs have been implemented in suburban areas.[6] For example, Oak Park's Housing Counseling Program (suburban Chicago) "seeks out liberal young whites and tries to settle them in mixed areas," and also tries to steer middle-class blacks from sections that have substantial black populations (Williams and Simons, 1977). The (Cleveland) Heights Area Project implemented by the Cleveland Jewish Community Federation[7] attempts to attract young Jewish families to this racially changing locality through low interest second mortgages (Varady, 1982). These two efforts have more potential for success than resident association activities because the two directly influence housing demand patterns. However, they are controversial because they are interpreted by some residents and outsiders as promoting black exclusion. As a result, it is unlikely that they will be replicated widely.

Improved prospects for neighborhood stabilization programs in racially changing communities will require better knowledge of the underlying factors affecting moving decisions of white and black residents in these communities. The author's 1979 study of white outmigration decisions from the racially changing Wynnefield community of Philadelphia is one of the few examples of this type of research. White panic moves were due to perceptions of a growing black population and concerns about violent street crime.

There have been few comparable studies of middle-class black moving and repair decisions. The limited available research suggests that middle-class blacks relocate to avoid problems associated with low-income ghettos. Vandell (1981), using 1960 and 1970 census data for St. Louis and Houston, found that transitional and, to a less extent, nonwhite neighborhoods succeeded to low-income neighborhoods faster than white ones. Katzman's 1983 literature review implied that there has been significant black flight from central city public schools. Both of these trends reflect a desire among middle-class blacks to avoid the debilitating effects of contact with lower class families (Clay, 1979). The preceding assertions have to be considered tentative, however, since they are not based on empirical data at the household level.

2. ETHNICITY AND NEIGHBORHOOD VIABILITY. Schoenberg and Rosenbaum's (1980) comparative analysis of five communities in St. Louis supports dual market theory showing that some communities with an aging housing stock do not experience physical and social decline.

Of the communities studied, the Hill, a prototypical Italian-American community, was clearly the most stable and viable. Most of the residents shared a common heritage with institutional life focused on the Catholic church. The Hill's viability was reflected in the strong patterns of block watchers. Strangers walking through the community were easily noticed and observed. Crime rates were much lower than in nearby communities. In addition, residents attached a great deal of importance to the neighborhood's appearance and to adequate garbage disposal. Finally, the neighborhood was able to maintain its homogeneity by controlling the housing market. Openings were usually filled within the community and were rarely listed in the newspaper or by realtors.

The Hill is one of the many examples of white ethnic communities that have experienced upgrading, physical improvement with the existing population in place (Clay, 1979). During the early 1960s this neighborhood began to experience the early signs of physical blight along its boundaries. Church leaders concerned about the problem organized Hill 2000, an improvement group. It was highly successful in raising funds through a series of street festivals and used the funds for an innovative rehabilitation program which reimbursed families for property improvements. Impressionistic evidence indicates that the effort to stem blight succeeded. Furthermore, during the 1970s the socioeconomic standing of the community rose in relation to others in St. Louis (Leven et al., 1976). It is unclear whether the improved economic position reflected the return of children raised in the community or the inmigration of working-class families from outside the area.

Upgrading efforts in communities like the Hill have presented bright prospects because they can build on the area's strengths (the population stability) and focus on the more manageable goal of improving physical conditions. The residents' concern for property upkeep and neighborhood appearance assures the continued maintenance of housing improvements.

Policymakers face a serious dilemma as to whether to support upgrading efforts in white ethnic communities. The homogeneous populations in these areas reflect both voluntary self-segregation by whites and overt discrimination against outsiders (see, for example, Wireman, 1984). It is questionable whether government should support these patterns of exclusivity. A case, however, can be made for doing so since such homogeneous neighborhoods are not inconsistent with the greater heterogeneous community or set of neighborhoods. Furthermore, the stability of these areas helps to maintain the city's tax base. Finally, the continued existence of these ethnic areas helps to make the city a more interesting and colorful place for visitors and residents alike.

3. ON THE INEVITABILITY OF NEIGHBORHOOD DECLINE. The existence of hundreds of gentrifying neighborhoods in cities across the

United States refutes the widely accepted belief that, once a neighborhood begins to decline, it is inevitable that it will proceed through the full cycle of deterioration leading ultimately to massive abandonment. Changing tastes for urban living and a desire to be closer to the central business district are among the underlying causes of the interest in this type of area by white collar professionals. Those who have written about gentrification have portrayed it as a form of invasion and succession, with middle-class families pushing out lower class and working-class families. It is assumed that the process involves intergroup conflict and that complete turnover to a middle-class population is inevitable (London and Palen, 1984, p. 9). If these assumptions are correct, then upgrading efforts by long time residents are futile because they will be displaced, whether or not physical upgrading occurs.

In reality, the above assumptions implied by the concept of invasion and succession have not always been supported. In Lafayette Park, St. Louis (Schoenberg and Rosenbaum, 1980), middle-class inmigration was not accompanied by displacement because of the availability of sufficient vacant homes. Middle and working-class families in the Hyde Park section of the same city lobbied together for historic district designation, the former out of a desire to preserve the housing, and the latter to retain as many of the working-class families as possible. Similarly, many of the working-class residents of the Melville Park section of Boston welcomed middle-class inmigration as a positive sign for the future of the community (Hollister, 1978). It is unknown whether these neighborhoods in St. Louis and Boston remained mixed, with both gentrifiers and new residents, or whether they underwent complete turnover to middle-class. Thus, the literature provides inadequate guidelines as to whether gentrification and upgrading can occur simultaneously within the same community.

The challenge for policymakers is to promote neighborhood changes that will benefit both groups. To do so, it will be necessary to design policies that reduce to a minimum the displacement of lower income families through, for example, condominium conversion legislation, loans to enable low-income families to make improvements, programs to help renters become owners, and counseling to prevent the loss of property. For a detailed discussion of such antidisplacement policies, see U.S.

Department of Housing and Urban Development, 1981. In order for gentrification to benefit inner city schools, it will be necessary to increase the numbers of public school families moving into and remaining in these areas. Orfield (1981) suggests a concerted program involving parents, neighborhood organizations, and local school districts to enroll white children in the local public schools, but there has been little research on this type of effort.

Recent Writings on Neighborhood Upgrading

A growing literature is emerging on the efforts of residents to stem decline and achieve physical improvements. As shown below, most of these writers (Clay, Downs, Goetze, Ahlbrandt) are optimistic about the prospects for reversing patterns of decline. Kolodny, however, is pessimistic, based on the limited ability of the government to influence population shifts.

Phillip Clay (1979, 1980, 1983) is probably cited more often than any other social scientist in his claims for the feasibility of improvement efforts by existing residents. In reality, his writings provide a mixed picture regarding the feasibility of the process. As indicated in the 1979 book, most of his work on upgrading is drawn from a 1977 mailed questionnaire survey sent to 225 key respondents in the thirty largest U.S. cities with a 35 percent response rate. In addition, site visits were made to nine large cities. Interviews with officials were supplemented by available secondary data. Because of the subjective methodology, the results should be considered tentative.

There were forty-eight instances of incumbent upgrading and fifty-seven of gentrification. But it would be a mistake to infer that incumbent upgrading occurred almost as frequently as gentrification. First, it is unclear how the thirty-five percent response rate biased the results, since no information is presented on the characteristics of cities that responded and those that did not. Second, since the book did not include a copy of the survey, it is unclear what criteria were used by public officials to identify examples of successful incumbent upgrading. Some of the officials may have classified neighborhoods as experiencing upgrading based solely on whether significant *efforts* were taking place.

The book and some of the subsequent articles based upon it offer a confusing picture on the prospects for successful upgrading in low-income and minority communities. Early in the book, Clay notes that a large number of low-income communities, many black, had substantially reversed their decline. He reinforces this point on page 77, noting that "neighborhood revival in even very deteriorated areas is feasible." Contrast these two assertions with two others in the book. He indicates that the most visible successes in upgrading have occurred in stable white ethnic working-class communities, which is consistent with the literature on dual markets reviewed earlier. In subsequent pages, he suggests tht black communities that have experienced racial transition, particularly those with high proportions of renters and high proportions of multifamily unit buildings, have poor prospects for achieving upgrading. In a later article, Clay (1980) dropped this factor, the neighborhood racial context, as an obstacle to successful upgrading. Was this due to the contradictions implicit in the 1979 text? The 1979 book does, however, raise an important question which has not been examined in later research: are the prospects for upgrading better in racially changing areas containing few renters and few multifamily unit buildings?

Myers and Binder (1977), using a similar approach, also emphasized the feasibility of neighborhood upgrading, even in racially changing communities. Interviews were conducted with public and private officials in six neighborhoods in three cities. This overly impressionistic methodology led to inaccurate conclusions regarding the feasibility of upgrading in Mt. Auburn, a racially changing inner-city community in Cincinnati. Myers and Binder assert (page 21) that the Mt. Auburn Good Housing Foundation, with considerable governmental financial assistance, was successful in rescuing this neighborhood "from physical decay and social disintegration." A recent demographic study of the community (McCray, 1985), questions this assumption. Although the large gap in median income between the city and the community has narrowed somewhat, property values and rents have continued to decline relative to the city, and vacancy rates have continued to rise. Furthermore, the limited statistical evidence of

improvement that is shown reflects gentrification in one part of
the community (Prospect Hill), rather than the results of
upgrading efforts in the poor black section.

Anthony Downs (1980, 1981; see also Public Affairs Counseling, 1975), like Phillip Clay and Phyllis Myers, is optimistic about
the prospects for neighborhood conservation programs based on
an analysis of theories of neighborhood decline. Neighborhoods
are seen to move through a life cycle from healthy (stage 1) to
nonviable (stage 5). Unlike Birch, Downs argues that public
policies can be used to stop and reverse the process of decline, as
long as intervention occurs early enough in the deterioration process.

Downs proposes physical programs like code enforcement
and street improvements for areas in these early stages of decline
(1980, p. 530). "Not only can such public spending help arrest
some decay in itself, but it may also induce private investors—especially people who already own property there— . . .
to increase *their* spending on upgrading." Downs does not provide
any support for the latter assertion. Nor is it clear how these
physical programs would deal with the underlying social causes
of population decline (e.g., racial and ethnic shifts). Downs is not
the only optimist, however, with regard to the influence of public
programs.

Goetze (1976, 1979, 1980) criticizes Downs's single continuum
or linear model of neighborhood change as overly simplistic. The
model, according to Goetze, incorrectly implies that revitalization
is reverse filtering, whereas a number of possible patterns are
possible. Some neighborhoods may upgrade gradually, while
others may upgrade quickly.

In contrast to earlier models of decline which stress housing
conditions, Goetze's includes two dimensions: housing, and
market perceptions. This framework highlights the fact that the
most rapid upgrading has often occurred in neighborhoods with
poor physical conditions but with high levels of confidence among
current and prospective residents.

Goetze recommends government efforts to influence the
public image of marginal neighborhoods (e.g., through posters,
newspaper stories, or television programs). It is asserted that, in
the past, the media overemphasized negative stories like crime

which reinforced unfounded fears and concerns about these areas.

The latter assertion is incorrect. Neighborhood racial change research reviewed above suggests that these fears were probably realistic in terms of what was occurring or was likely to occur based on ghetto expansion patterns. Efforts to present only the positive side of a community are not likely to fool residents who have lived through the process in another community or who have observed it happen elsewhere.

Ahlbrandt and Cunningham (1979) also emphasize the feasibility of upgrading, based on an empirical study of investment and mobility decisions in Pittsburgh. Both types of decisions were influenced by the social fabric of the area. This implied that neighborhood decline was caused by a weakening of the social fabric, and that city funded organizing efforts could reverse decline.

The authors do not explore sufficiently the factors responsible for a weakening social fabric. Had they done so, racial and socioeconomic shifts would probably have been shown to be important. Ahlbrandt and Cunningham greatly overstate the ability of local government to manage population shifts. The assertion (page 150) that "flight from the city to suburbs is 'not an insurmountable problem' " is contradicted by their own statistical results. When a suburban sample was asked their reasons for moving out of the city, only 15 percent cited things like crime or deteriorating neighborhoods that the city could affect. Furthermore, the assertion that cities could stabilize racially changing neighborhoods through community organization (i.e., "bridge communication gaps btween groups") flies in the face of hundreds of unsuccessful stabilization efforts in racially changing communities across the country.

Survey results from Boston (Bratt, 1983) contradict Ahlbrandt and Cunningham's optimism about upgrading efforts. "Type of people" was the most important consideration in residents' assessments of neighborhood qualities, reflecting a strong quest for socioeconomic and racial homogeneity. This implies a limited role for government (p. 144), since "there is nothing that the city can do to make good neighbors."

A common theme in most of the works cited in this section is that neighborhood upgrading is feasible even if it involves population stabilization. Kolodny correctly (1983) questions this assumption. Noting that neighborhood change involves both push and pull sources, he stresses that even if local government could affect pushes, it could not affect such pulls as the existence of homogeneous suburban areas. Hence, there is little that government *can* do to prevent population shifts. Nor, according to Kolodny, *should* government even try to manage such shifts, because such programs are inequitable. Neighborhood stabilization programs work against the interests of home-seeking poor families who benefit from filtering and actually support the interests of middle-class families. Local governments should attempt to maintain and enhance the quality of life for residents, whomever they are. Policymakers should promote neighborhood stabilization by addressing the systemic causes of decline, such as inner-city poverty, racial discrimination, and so forth.

Three weaknesses in Kolodny's otherwise strong argument should be noted. First, he exaggerates the benefits of the filtering process for the poor. The improvements that they attain by relocating away from the city center are often temporary, as these areas slide toward nonviability. Second, it is difficult to separate programs that promote stabilization from those oriented to enhancing the quality of life for residents, whoever they are. For example, how would improvements in the local public schools be classified?

Finally, the research literature is far less conclusive than Kolodny's article would suggest regarding the lack of impact of government programs on population changes. On the one hand, and in support of Kolodny, the few empirical studies on the subject using metropolitan samples have shown that the quality of public services has little, if any, impact on the decision of when to move (Goodman, 1978; Varady, 1983). On the other hand, there is broad consensus among economists on the importance of public services, such as the local public schools, in affecting family moving decisions (see, for example, Armor, 1980; Jud, 1985; and Kain and Quigley, 1970). The seeming inconsistency may reflect the fact that although these services do not have an impact on the decision of when to move, they do have an influence on where the household chooses to locate. It is conceivable, for example, that improvements in local public schools, including quotas to maintain a racial and social class balance (Orfield, 1981), might help to attract middle-income and white families to inner-city locations. Unfortunately, there has been very little empirical research on this second type of migration decision.

The Indirect Effects of Government Subsidized Housing Programs

In the past, policymakers have justified funding for housing programs based on the neighborhood spillover effects of these programs, such as higher property values in the immediate area (U.S. Senate Committee on Banking, Housing and Urban Affairs, 1977).[8] It is assumed that government housing programs could promote positive spillover effects on property values by reducing the degree of uncertainty among current and prospective homeowners. Specifically, visible improvements resulting from housing programs, combined with strategies to upgrade community services and facilities, could make nearby residents more optimistic about the neighborhood's future and therefore make them more likely to invest. These improvements could also modify lending patterns, thereby leading to higher levels of housing demand in the area.

There has been considerable debate among social scientists about the types of housing programs that will have the most pronounced impacts on surrounding property values. DeSalvo's research (1974, p. 271) suggests that the construction of new housing in low income areas will have a particularly marked effect on values when it replaces fire trap dwellings. Conversely, the improvement of standard housing in middle income areas will have a far less substantial impact on values. Goetze and Colton (1983, pp. 180–190) are skeptical, however, about the ability of federal housing programs in general to achieve neighborhood upgrading, which includes rising property values. Both the programs for new housing and the programs for existing housing of the 1960s tended to undermine neighborhood confidence and reduced the prospects for achieving revitalization. Goetze and Colton's work implies that only those housing strategies that are combined with programs to instill neighborhood confidence have a meaningful chance to promote revitalization. At the same time, it should be noted that the limited impact of the housing programs of the 1960s may have been due to problems in the way they were implemented rather than the absence of programs promoting neighborhood confidence, Had they been run better, they might have contributed to higher values.

There is considerably more consensus in the social science literature about two geographic or spatial aspects of the spillover phenomenon. First, there is agreement that programs concentrated on particular blocks and neighborhoods are more likely to have an impact on property values in the surrounding area (see, for example, Segal, 1977, p. 128). Second, there is considerable unanimity that the geographic impacts of most housing programs will be quite limited (Dear, Fincher and Currie, 1977; DeSalvo, 1974).

The research reviewed up to this point is largely theoretical. Empirical research through the mid-1970s dealt mostly with public housing and other forms of new construction and provided weak support for the hypothesized positive effects on values (see DeSalvo, 1974, and Nourse, 1976). This weak evidence is not surprising given the "common wisdom" that public housing reduces property values.

While not dealing directly with subsidized housing, two additional studies are relevant to the issue of the effects of upgrading on property values. Nourse (1976) found that social class factors (e.g., proximity to an expanding ghetto area) were more important than physical factors (e.g., age of housing) in explaining differences in property values between two suburban St. Louis municipalities. This strongly implied (p. 248) "that improvement in housing is unlikely to have an impact on neighborhood property values unless other market changes are present."

Li and Brown's recent study (1980) of the impact of microneighborhood variables on housing prices is also relevant to the spillover issue. Two characteristics were shown to be statistically significant predictors of prices: residential density and the percentage of persons 16 to 21, a very crude measure of crime and vandalism. In addition, there was a strong positive correlation between the visual quality of the site and home prices. These results imply that in neighborhoods with historic or otherwise attractive homes, housing rehabilitation programs could have positive spillover effects on surrounding properties. If these programs are to have the greatest possible effect, they need to be combined with strategies to deal with such neighborhood problems as high density, crime and vandalism.

Previous spillover research has overemphasized the importance of property values as a measure of program impact, a consequence of monitoring periods for such studies that are usually quite brief, only two to three years. Several recent studies of governmental and nongovernmental upgrading programs overcome this problem by analyzing other measures, including changes in the socioeconomic characteristics of the population, neighborhood investment, neighborhood appearance, all in addition to changes in property values. All of these programs attempt to stabilize the populations in these areas while improving physical conditions.

A. Neighborhood Housing Services

The Neighborhood Housing Services (NHS) model, one of the most frequently mentioned strategies for neighborhood preservation and stabilization, was originally created in Pittsburgh as a result of efforts by community activists and lenders. The Urban Reinvestment Task Force (composed of representatives of HUD, the Federal Home Loan Bank Board, the Federal Reserve System, the Federal Deposit Insurance Corporation, and the Comptroller of the Currency) has since initiated NHS programs throughout the country.

One of the unique features of NHS is the high degree of resident involvement in the operation of the program. Residents comprise a majority of board members. Presumably, this high degree of involvement benefits neighborhood preservation in a number of different ways (Goetze, 1979, 1980; Urban Systems, Research and Engineering, Inc., 1980). First, the inclusion of residents on the board improves the bureaucracy by insuring that the organization will remain committed to improvement rather than to institutional maintenance. Second, it creates a sense of trust among the partners (residents, lenders, and city officials), whereas previously an unbalanced power relationship existed.

Third, it creates a sense of control over local conditions. This sense of trust and control presumably "filters down" from community representatives to residents of the community. Finally, it helps to create a realistic set of expectations among residents and helps to raise their spirits.

Other components of the NHS model include: (1) local government participation through capital improvements and code enforcement programs; (2) the agreement of financial institutions to reinvest in the community by making market rate loans to qualified buyers and through contributions to the NHS to support operating costs; and (3) a high risk loan fund to families who cannot meet usual credit risk standards.

Although the NHS model has been widely viewed as successful in promoting upgrading (see, for example, Downs, 1981; Goetze, 1979), the available empirical evidence is far from convincing. Ahlbrandt and Brophy (1975) used a variety of data sources to compare changes in the Central North Side of Pittsburgh (the location of the first NHS) with four other communities which were similar with respect to population and housing characteristics but which were not experiencing significant revitalization activity. Although the results were somewhat mixed, they did seem to suggest that the Central North Side improved relative to the other neighborhoods, leading the authors to assert that the improvement stemmed from NHS activities. However, the communities may not have been sufficiently comparable to draw this conclusion. Ahlbrandt and Brophy indicate that sections of the Central North Side contained attractive and historically important housing. Therefore, the variation in rates of improvement may have been due to differences in the amenity value of the housing. Furthermore, the positive results may have been due to conditions idiosyncratic to Pittsburgh. For example, the fact that the city is hemmed in by hills makes inner-city areas more attractive than would otherwise be the case. Consequently, it would be a mistake to generalize from Pittsburgh to other cities. The Ahlbrandt and Brophy study is limited, however, in a more fundamental way: it does not directly test for the impact of the program or of components of the program on individual mobility and investment decisions, making it impossible to assess the effects of the program on nonparticipating families.

A more recent study (Pedone, 1982) of the NHS nationally by Urban Systems Research and Engineering Inc. (USR&E) did include tests for the spillovers hypothesis but little support was shown. This national study, basically similar to USR&E's study of the UHD to be discussed in the next chapter, was based on three waves of interviews with approximately 1,700 families in twenty neighborhoods, plus windshield survey data on these communities. The results exhibited no evidence of improvement among nonparticipating families. Being aware of the NHS, while not an NHS client, did not contribute to an increased likelihood of investing in home improvements when other background characteristics were controlled. Nor did such an awareness lead to a greater likelihood of remaining in these communities. The improvement in the NHS neighborhoods probably reflected broader housing market forces and would have occurred even if the NHS program had not been implemented (Pedone, 1982).

How can one reconcile the NHS's excellent reputation with the weak results in the USR&E study? First, it is conceivable that the program was in operation for too short a period to have measurable effects. However, the insignificant results may reflect the racial changes during the 1970s in many of the NHS communities where NHS programs were insufficient to counterbalance these population shifts. The results provide some support for the first explanation. The existence of racial change led to a decreased likelihood of investment among NHS residents. Pedone speculated that uncertainties about price trends made residents unwilling to invest. Unfortunately, the NHS data set did not include measures of the expected price trends, so it was impossible to test further for the validity of this explanation.

B. Lending Institutions

In the past, commercial banks and savings and loan institutions have been accused of "redlining" transitional and inner-city black areas. This occurs when bank officers draw red lines around areas and withhold mortgage and improvement loans from them. In recent years, some of these institutions have tried to change their image and have become involved in a variety of preservation/stabilization activities, with NHS being only one example (U.S. Department of Housing and Urban Development,

1979). The activities of the South Shore Bank and its holding institution, the Illinois Neighborhood Development Corporation, are perhaps the most far reaching and therefore worthy of detailed scrutiny.

The South Shore Bank sought to provide increased funds for creditworthy single family and multifamily building owners. It has also attempted "to be a catalyst for community revitalization activities by residents, other private actors and the public sector." An evaluation by the Woodstock Institute (1982) showed that these activities had a mixed record of success during the late 1970s. Property values, which had declined relative to the city during racial change in the early 1970s, increased relatively during the late 1970s. The increases were greatest in the areas with the largest number of loans. In addition, there was a dramatic increase in building permits and a decline in the proportion of tax delinquent multifamily buildings. On the other hand, the desired revitalization of the commercial district did not occur.

One of the major limitations of the evaluation is the lack of information provided on the extent of spillover effects from bank programs. For example, it is possible that most of the improvement in multifamily buildings occurred as a result of the South Shore Bank loans and that few other building owners improved their properties. Without evidence of such spillover effects, it is premature to consider the bank a catalyst in revitalization efforts. In addition, the analysis focused exclusively on economic and physical changes, and it ignored social and attitudinal shifts, such as changes in the incidence of public assistance, confidence levels, and so on. Although, crime was a serious problem in the community in the early 1970s (Molotch, 1972), this problem was virtually ignored in the Woodstock report. While it would be unrealistic to expect a bank lending program alone to affect all of these factors it nevertheless has to spark improvements in social, as well as physical, conditions. Upgrading efforts which focus on physical conditions alone are not likely to succeed in the long run.

Finally, the South Shore Bank model may not be easily replicable. It is probably unrealistic to expect other banks and holding companies primarily concerned with profit maximization to engage in the comprehensive programs of the South Shore Bank and to be satisfied with an "adequate" profit.

C. Neighborhood Strategy Areas—Section 8

The Neighborhood Strategy Area (NSA) demonstration was initiated by HUD in 1978 to strengthen neighborhood revitalization efforts by giving local governments control over Section 8 Substantial Rehabilitation allocations for use in target neighborhoods. In return, cities were to develop detailed revitalization plans for these neighborhoods, combining public and private housing and community development resources in a way that would meet all of the neighborhood's revitalization needs during the five-year demonstration period (Bleakly et al., 1983, p. 1). A total of sixteen cities containing 150 NSA's were selected for the demonstration. The assessment of the NSA demonstration focused on a sample of thirty neighborhoods in twenty cities.

The results were mixed. The program had only a limited impact on prices;" . . . while NSAs are not improving vis-a-vis the rest of the SMSA [Standard Metropolitan Statistical Area], they do not appear to be declining either" (Bleakly et al, 1982, p. 15). The unanswered question is whether a slowdown in the rate of decline is an acceptable measure of success.

The program had a greater impact on neighborhood physical conditions. Those neighborhoods where the rehabilitation process associated with the program had moved furthest along were the ones with the greatest amount of *overall physical improvement*. It is unclear how much of this improvement was due to the direct effects of the program (e.g., better street maintenance by city agencies), and how much was due to the indirect effects on residents (e.g., rehabilitation leading to greater confidence and, in turn, better property upkeep). Without the latter type of evidence, it is impossible to fully assess the adequacy of this strategy.

The NSA-Section 8 evaluation did not relate measures of program activity to individual household mobility or investment behavior, as was the case in the NHS study. An equally serious limitation was the lack of attention to the population shifts occurring in these areas. Bleakly et al. (1982, p. 19) note that "the neighborhoods selected for the NSA program appear to be those which are experiencing significant population shifts: the total population in the NSA is declining while the black population is growing." The research did not examine the effects, if any, of the program in allaying concerns of residents about these shifts; nor did the evaluation examine the influence of racial shifts on the effectiveness of the program.

D. Community Development Block Grants

HUD's Community Development Block Grant (CDBG) program is the federal government's main housing improvement program. Created in 1974, it seeks to provide a suitable living environment and expanded economic opportunities, principally for persons of low and moderate income. Most of the money goes to 550 metropolitan areas and 84 large counties which, because of their size, physical conditions and financial situation, are entitled to CDBG funds.

CDBG funds can be used for a wide range of activities: acquiring property, rehabilitating single family or multifamily homes, and providing public services to the community. For a detailed description of some of the more innovative programs implemented using CDBG funds, see U.S. Department of Housing and Urban Development (HUD), 1983.

The CDBG program employs the targeting approach. For housing rehabilitation, a city usually identifies target areas that range from a few blocks to a whole census tract and awards grants, loans, or a combination of the two to selected homeowners in these areas. It is assumed that the concentration of funds in these areas acts as a catalyst to encourage nonqualifying homeowners to improve their properties.

Does this actually occur? McFarland (1984) sought to answer this question by comparing changes in housing quality from 1970 to 1980 between six census tracts in Springfield Illinois' CDBG target area and two other comparable tracts which did not receive rehabilitation funds. The results do not support the hypothesized effects of targeting. While four of the six CDBG tracts experienced improvements in housing quality, both of the control tracts experienced improvement. Obviously, other factors besides housing rehabilitation were responsible for the improvements.

The above results should be considered tentative. It is well known that correlations based on aggregated areal units of analysis such as census tracts may be different from the correlations when individuals or families are taken as the unit of analysis. This is known as the ecological fallacy. The Community Development Strategies Evaluation by the University of Pennsylvania for the U.S. Department of HUD made a contribution to the literature by linking data on specific grants and loans to individual respondents in the household survey. This made it possible to test whether there was an increased tendency to remain and invest as a result of the level and types of assisted rehabilitation in the vicinity of the household. The study was based on two waves of household surveys between 1978 and 1979 with approximately 4,000 households in nine cities, including those receiving rehabilitation assistance and those not, as well as neighborhood windshield surveys completed by trained observers.

The results (R. Ginsberg, 1983) supported the existence of spillovers in home improvement decisions. Higher levels of rehabilitation grants within the respondent's grid square (i.e., within one-sixteenth of a mile) generated additional repairs. It is not clear why assistance in the form of grants had more impact than assistance in the form of loans. In contrast, rehabilitation activity and neighborhood conditions had little impact on mobility.

Although the CDBG evaluation was one of the most sophisticated studies of neighborhood upgrading, relatively little attention was given to the neighborhood racial context. While the regression models did include a measure of the racial composition of the census tract in 1980, the models did not include measures of change between 1970 and 1980. Indicators of change have usually been found to be more influential in mobility decisions than measures of the composition at one point in time. Furthermore, the survey did not include indicators of concerns about racial and race related shifts, variables likely to be important in explaining mobility and repair decisions.

E. Code Enforcement

A number of racially changing suburban communities have used code enforcement programs to try to stabilize their housing and populations during or immediately after racial transition. The two efforts that have been evaluated, in Pasadena and University

City (St. Louis), require that each vacant unit pass code inspection before being rented or sold, and University City further established a maximum number of residents for each housing unit. The purpose of both programs was to reassure residents that racial changes would not result in the doubling up of families in apartment units, causing a decline in housing quality.

Neither evaluation involved analysis at the household level. However, the results are positive enough to suggest that code enforcement might play a role in stabilization efforts. Meier (1983), studying Pasadena, used regression analysis and a multiple time series design to test two measures of program activity (extensiveness, that is, the number of units inspected per 1,000 and the degree of compliance with code) on housing quality, as indicated by price trends. He found that the program had a positive impact on prices in middle-class and, to a lesser extent, lower middle-class areas.

Leven et al. (1976) obtained comparable results for University City using a less sophisticated statistical approach. The population turnover rates, after increasing in 1967, remained the same or decreased afterwards. The decline in prices during the 1960s ceased, and the socioeconomic ranking of tracts remained the same. The program, however, had little impact on racial shifts, and the proportion of blacks continued to rise throughout the community. Leven et al. (p. 133) notes that the relative stability of the community may have been due to other factors besides the program.

> The (code enforcement) ordinance may have been assisted by a shortage of housing finance to fund white flight. The shortage was a result of the then effective state ceiling on mortgage interest rates at 8 percent when market rates nationally were higher.

F. Neighborhood Confidence Project

The purpose of the Neighborhood Confidence Project in Boston was to stimulate positive self-fulfilling prophecies in three neighborhoods: Dorchester, Roxbury, and Jamaica Plain. More specifically, the project sought to: (1) encourage owners to remain, (2) encourage renters and those outside the community to buy homes, and (3) change the attitudes of real estate brokers. Specific activities of the Project included the production of a television documentary, brochures and posters, and the counseling of buyers.

Goetze (1979) citing studies by Blaine (1973) and Rugo (1979) asserts that the Project was successful, noting that the program in Jamaica Plain raised confidence levels and improved community appearance. Unfortunately, he did not present evidence in the book to support the conclusion, nor did he indicate the approach used to test for program impact. More specifically, it is unclear whether any attempt was made to compare attitudinal and physical changes in Jamaica Plain with shifts in similar communities. Since efforts to secure copies of Blaine's master's thesis and Rugo's report to the Boston Redevelopment Authority proved unsuccessful, it was not possible to evaluate their methods.

The most detailed study of the Project by Hollister (1978) provides weak evidence of success. Three hundred seventy-six interviews were conducted with residents in 1977 and forty in-depth interviews were completed in 1978. The evaluation focused on the level of satisfaction of the respondents with products of the Project such as the television documentary. However, this was far too narrow a measure of success. No attempt was made to compare population and housing shifts in the above three neighborhoods with control areas, nor was an attempt made to assess the impact of the project in holding or attracting new residents to these areas. Both analyses are necessary to judge success.

The case studies of particular neighborhoods in Boston in Hollister's report highlight the impracticality of using public relations as a primary vehicle for upgrading. Confidence levels were highest in stable white ethnic neighborhoods like Minot (a mostly Irish area) and were lowest in racially changing areas like Draper. Respondents' expectations regarding their neighborhoods seemed to be realistic in light of what was actually happening and what was likely to happen, given the patterns of expansion of the black and Hispanic ghettos. Publicity efforts, like those in this Project have limited prospects for success where residents have such legitimate fears.

The correlation between racial homogeneity and confidence

does not suggest useful policy guidelines. As mentioned earlier, it would be inappropriate for the government to try to achieve racial homogeneity as part of a policy for achieving neighborhood upgrading.

Conclusion

Although orthodox economic theory has been influential in the development of housing policy, it is inadequate as a basis for neighborhood preservation policy because it does not identify the primary causes of decline. The assumption by many economists that the aging of the housing stock is the key factor in explaining neighborhood decline is clearly unrealistic. Furthermore, it has led to an overemphasis on cosmetic housing improvements as the main thrust of neighborhood upgrading efforts.

Some neighborhoods have experienced a more rapid decline than would be expected on the basis of the age of the housing alone. In many of these areas, decline can be explained by racial and economic shifts. To be successful, neighborhood stabilization efforts must address the underlying causes of these population shifts.

On the other hand, many other neighborhoods, often white ethnic ones, have remained viable despite an aging stock. The viability of these areas is a product of social rather than economic variables, where perceived patterns of interdependence lead to high levels of property upkeep. Finally, existing research questions the widely held belief that once gentrification begins, complete turnover to a middle-class population is inevitable, making upgrading efforts by long-time residents futile.

The prospects for upgrading vary by community type. They are bright in white ethnic areas where upgrading can focus on the manageable goal of physical improvements. On the other hand, the potential for improvement is uncertain in areas that have experienced or are experiencing income and/or racial change where upgrading requires stabilizing the social class and possibly the racial composition of the population. Past efforts to achieve stabilization by working through local resident associations have not been successful.

Unfortunately, HUD officials either ignored or were unaware of the point that success depends on community type when they prepared the most recent *President's National Urban Policy Report* (U.S. Department of Housing and Urban Development, 1984, p. 67). Echoing Clay's 1979 study, the report states that both low-and moderate-income areas are experiencing "incumbent upgrading," often as a result of organizing efforts by churches and civic organizations. The implication is that virtually any neighborhood can experience upgrading with the right type of organizing efforts. This implication is, of course, unwarranted, since most of the examples of upgrading have been in stable white ethnic communities. The *Report's* authors apparently overlooked Clay's statement that racial transition is an obstacle to successful upgrading.

With the exception of Kolodny, those who have written about neighborhood preservation during the past ten years or so have been overly optimistic about the prospects for upgrading because they have overlooked the seemingly intractable issue of how to arrest racial and social class changes. The policies that have been proposed—better public relations, code enforcement, community organizing—fail to address the underlying cause of decline in these areas: that is, the pressure of black and later low-income housing demand from expanding ghetto areas. Until these underlying causes are addressed, the prospects for stabilization and upgrading are limited.

Recent federal neighborhood preservation demonstrations have been similarly flawed by a lack of attention to racial and social class changes. For example, the South Shore Bank study (Chicago, Woodstock Institute, 1982) virtually ignored street crime even though this was one of the most serious community problems during the 1970s. It should be clear from the preceding that, to date, neighborhood preservation efforts have been defined too narrowly around physical housing conditions and property values. Unless the controversial issues of race and social class changes are dealt with explicitly, the prospects for long-range improvement in these areas will be minimal.

The empirical results from the more sophisticated demonstrations (NHS, CDBG) are likely to be discouraging to policymakers.

None of these evaluations provides evidence that these programs could hold or attract middle-income families thereby slowing neighborhood decline.

Recent research suggests three possible scenarios for achieving population stabilization and, in turn, neighborhood upgrading.

1. STABILIZATION THROUGH GENTRIFICATION. The inmigration of middle-class families to an area with attractive housing may reinforce existing upgrading efforts by raising confidence levels. A variety of factors (high rates of ownership, large numbers of vacant homes for gentrifying families) may prevent complete turnover from working to middle class. An unanswered question from previous studies is whether the presence of an established black population would decrease interest levels among prospective white gentrifiers.

2. SOCIAL CLASS STABILIZATION WITHOUT RACIAL STABILIZATION. Clay's research implies that the prospects for upgrading are relatively good in racially changing areas with a low proportion of renters and a low proportion of multifamily unit buildings. That is, these areas may achieve physical improvements with the middle-class black population in place. Since much of the racial transition in recent years has been in attractive suburban and suburban-type areas, the incidence of this type of social class stabilization may increase. More, however, needs to be known about the mobility and repair decisions of middle-class blacks to assess the feasibility of this strategy.

3. RACIAL AND SOCIAL CLASS STABILIZATION. Although the prospects for achieving stable racial integration along the edge of ghetto areas are generally poor, there may be situations where stabilization is feasible, perhaps where the housing is attractive to middle-income families and modestly priced in relation to what is available in nearby areas. Government programs which improve residents' expectations concerning population and housing changes may improve the prospects for stabilization.

Unfortunately, the revitalization literature provides inadequate guidance regarding the prospects for these three types of stabilization. Those who have proposed specific upgrading mechanisms (e.g., code enforcement, publicity, community organizing, concentrated rehabilitation activity) typically have not indicated their likely success in different types of communities (predominantly white, racially changing). Empirical research on upgrading programs has been deficient in two critical ways. First, most of the research has relied on neighborhood level data, which is inherently weak for assessing program impact. Second, the few studies which have gathered household level data have failed to examine how the neighborhood socioeconomic context affects program impact. For example, do particular upgrading strategies have more of an impact on mobility and investment decisions in stable middle-income communities than in those experiencing income decline? Are middle-income mobility decisions more sensitive than those of lower income householders to variations in the quality of public services? If supported, improved services may help to promote social class stabilization, if not racial stabilization.

This book seeks to improve understanding of how governments can promote demographic stabilization and reverse physical deterioration in declining communities through analysis of moving and home improvement decisions of nonparticipating families in urban homesteading neighborhoods. The analysis seeks to assess the impact of homesteading activity and other aspects of the residential environment on these two interrelated decisions. Chapter 2 describes urban homesteading and the Urban Homesteading Demonstration data sets on which the analysis in later chapters is based.

Chapter 2

Urban Homesteading

Historical Antecedents

When the term "urban homesteading" was introduced in the 1970s, it received a great deal of favorable publicity. Commentators and analysts were highly optimistic about its potential for conserving the urban housing stock and for revitalizing declining inner-city neighborhoods. One reason for the favorable publicity and the optimism was the seeming similarity between this new program and rural homesteading of the nineteenth century.

Although the analogy between types of homesteading is not precise, the earlier rural programs do offer important lessons for the current one.[1] The original homesteading program of 1862 provided families with either 80 or 160 acres of land, depending on location, on the condition that they improve it and remain on it for at least five years. Two hundred eighty-seven million acres of land in the Midwest and West were settled through this program, benefitting hundreds of thousands of homesteaders. As the more fertile lands in the Midwest were settled, it became progressively more difficult to attract homesteading families. Consequently, in 1912 the residence requirement was relaxed. Nevertheless, interest in the program continued to wane. The program ended in the mid-1930s with the land being returned to the federal government.

Concurrent with the demise of the original homesteading program, a new program, subsistence homesteading, was introduced as part of the New Deal. The program, part of a broader effort to decentralize the urban industrial population, provided low interest loans to unemployed workers to purchase these homesteads. Unlike the 1862 program, the government played a direct role in the construction of dwellings, the purchase of livestock and equipment, and so forth. The Division of Subsistence Homesteads in the Department of Interior was instrumental in creating three types of "colonies": communities of part-time farmers near industrial employment, rural colonies of resettled farmers, and villages with newly resettled industries.

Roosevelt, in central New Jersey, was an example of the first and most successful type (Hughes and Bleakly, 1975). It consisted of 200 skilled Jewish needleworkers who attempted to become self-sufficient through a combination of part-time employment in a cooperative garment factory and subsistence farming. The project was plagued by high costs and inefficient labor, which led to the factory's closing after a year. Nevertheless, the residential portion of the project remained and still exists today as an attractive suburb.

Three lessons may be drawn from the earlier forms of rural homesteading to the current urban efforts. First, the earlier efforts emphasize the importance of location. The 1862 program was successful in the fertile Midwest but was a failure in the arid West. The most successful subsistence programs were those in the suburbs of expanding metropolitan areas. The experience implies selecting neighborhoods for homesteading which are in the early stages of the decline process.

Second, earlier efforts highlight the difficulties of reaching the most needy as part of homesteading efforts. The 1862 program was unsuccessful in attracting urban poor because of the high costs of relocating and setting up a new farm. The program attracted homesteaders who were modestly successful Easterners who had sold their farms to make the move. Similarly, although the subsistence homesteading program was designed to assist the most needy, in practice, the selection favored those whose resources contributed to the financial stability of the colony. The past, therefore, "provides a warning to urban homestead experiments that the income and assets of potential homesteaders may be the most critical factor determining their success or failure" (Urban Systems, Research and Engineering, Inc., 1977, p. 23).

Third, the individual's chances for success in both earlier programs were tied to public efforts. Although there is some truth to the notion that success on the frontier was a function of personal initiative, the most successful homesteads were those located near railroads constructed on land provided by the federal government. The Subsistence Homesteading Program provided a far more comprehensive set of public improvements and social services which helped to increase the individual colony's chances for survival. The present Urban Homesteading program's success may therefore be tied to support efforts by local government (providing better schools, repaired playgrounds, improved police protection, and so on).

Local Homesteading Programs

The growing problem of housing abandonment during the late 1960s led to the idea of applying homesteading principles to urban housing problems. The federal government had contributed to this problem through the flawed 235 Program. Under this program low-income families were able to secure single family homes with very low down payments and long-term low interest loans. When owners realized these homes required major repairs they could not afford, dwellings were abandoned. As a result, the U.S. Department of Housing and Urban Development became one of the largest slum landlords in the country.

The first urban homesteading program began in 1973 in Wilmington, Delaware, with programs in Philadelphia and Baltimore established shortly thereafter. These early programs received tremendous publicity, homesteading advocates citing not only the program's ability to conserve the housing stock but also its potential for stabilizing declining neighborhoods.

> The cities . . . have embarked on an exciting venture to stabilize declining neighborhoods through urban homesteading. . . . We at the National Urban Coalition believe that homesteading has great potential as a force for neighborhood revitalization . . . urban homesteading offers us the opportunity to reclaim whole neighborhoods and to meet the housing needs of the people most affected by abandonment—the poor. (National Urban Coalition, 1974, p. 5).

However, an evaluation of these early efforts showed that homesteading would not be a panacea for urban housing problems (Hughes and Bleakly, 1975). First, insufficient attention was given in these early efforts to "take out mechanisms," i.e., homesteaders lacked assurance that they would be able to recoup their financial investment, as well as the labor they had put into their properties. Second, homesteading's appeal as a "noninstitutional" approach was deceptive. To be successful, homesteading required significant participation by the local government. Cities would need to monitor the supply of vacant and abandoned housing as an ongoing process so as to acquire vacant houses while they were still salvageable. Third, in contrast to the widespread image of homesteading as a solution to the low-income housing problem, the program was only suitable for those with the means to afford rehabilitation. As was the case in the earlier subsistence program, "homesteading is not, and without massive government aid cannot be, truly a housing program for low-income persons" (Hughes and Bleakly, 1975, p. 194). Finally, homesteading's success was dependent on neighborhood improvements by local government. Unless these were made, homesteaders were unlikely to take the risks in making expensive housing repairs.

Hughes and Bleakly emphasized the need to measure the neighborhood effects of the program. Property tax adjustments were seen necessary to make homesteading economically feasible for participants. Since the adjustments increased the program's cost to city residents, the program could be justified only if it led to higher values for surrounding properties and increased the city's tax base. Hughes and Bleakly completed their evaluation too early in the history of these municipal efforts to measure the program's neighborhood impacts. However, later research on HUD's Urban Homesteading Demonstration addressed this issue.

The Federal Government's Urban Homesteading Demonstration

The extensive publicity surrounding local homesteading programs increased congressional interest in the concept. HUD's Urban Homesteading Demonstration (UHD) was enacted as Section

810 of the Community Development Act of 1974. It permitted HUD to transfer federally owned one- to four-family houses to cities using such properties as part of a homesteading program. Five million dollars was authorized to permit cities to acquire these properties, and Section 312 loan funds were made available in conjunction with these efforts.

HUD's Office of Policy Development and Research was given the responsibility of running the Demonstration. Twenty-three cities were selected to participate in the first round of the Demonstration announced in October 1975.[2] Fifteen additional cities were selected in May 1977. In December 1978, the status of the program was changed from that of a Demonstration to an operating program.

At about the time that the UHD began, HUD chose Urban Systems, Research and Engineering, Inc. (USR&E) to evaluate the program in the original 23 cities "(1) to assess the success of homesteading as a strategy to rehabilitate the housing stock in urban neighborhoods, and (2) to measure the impact of the homesteading effort on the target neighborhoods" (USR&E, 1983, p. 4). The longitudinal evaluation included three waves of interviews with 812 of the original homesteaders, three waves of interviews with 1,754 nonparticipating households in UHD neighborhoods, and three waves of windshield surveys of housing and block conditions.[3] These two data sets (neighborhood residents and windshield surveys), along with census data, were combined into one set which was used in the analysis for this book.

Cities selected to participate in the Demonstration were given a great deal of flexibility in administering local homesteading programs. However, two HUD directives increased the potential for achieving neighborhood stabilization. First, HUD required that cities choose "declining neighborhoods which are not severely blighted and have the potential of regaining their viability" (USR&E, 1977, Vol. 2, 1978, p. v). Second, urban homesteading was viewed as only "one element in a coordinated program of neighborhood stabilization." The provision of other supportive services (discussed later) was supposed to increase the prospects for successful stabilization.

The following section summarizing the Demonstration experience is divided into two parts: (1) the selection of neighborhoods, properties and homesteaders, and (2) the relative success of the Demonstration in improving housing conditions and in stabilizing neighborhoods.

1.Selecting neighborhoods, properties and homesteaders.

a. NEIGHBORHOODS. Cities used similar criteria in designating their target areas: a high number of HUD-owned vacant properties, a concentration of other city services in the area, neighborhood conditions (e.g., relatively high income and homeownership levels), an active neighborhood organization, and prior existence as an administratively defined area. In some cases, the neighborhood was already designated as a Community Development Target area or a Neighborhood Housing Services (NHS) area. In other cases, the neighborhood boundaries were defined to be coterminous with the census tract.

The UHD neighborhoods varied widely in population size from 1,000 in South Bend's Riverside Manor to over 100,000 in Milwaukee's Northwest Side.[4] It is important to provide a sense of perspective on the relationship between urban homesteading and the UHD neighborhoods. On the average, homesteading properties comprised 2 percent of the total, and homesteaders constituted 1 percent of the total population.

The neighborhoods selected did appear to meet the HUD criteria. That they had begun to experience decline is shown by decreases in income levels and home sale prices in relation to national figures (USR&E, 1978, p. 62–63). These were neighborhoods, however, was the rapid racial change. During the reverse patterns of decline. Both the rates of homeownership (65 percent) and average income levels ($10,675) were fairly high. The most striking demographic characteristic of these neighborhoods, however, was the rapid racial change. During the 1970 to 1977 period, the proportion of blacks rose from 45 to 65 percent. "In only 13 of the 40 neighborhoods did the number of black families increase by less than five percent of the area's population, and in six of the neighborhoods, the percentage of the population which is black increased by over 40 percent" (page 66).

USR&E did not have available 1980 census information when the preceding portraits of the UHD neighborhoods were developed. The availability of this information along with the 1970 data highlights the racial shifts that occurred during the 1970s (Table 2.1). During this period the average neighborhood experienced a 21 percent increase in the proportion of blacks and was about three-fifths (61 percent) black at the end of the decade. The most rapid increases occurred in two Chicago neighborhoods: Austin and Roseland. Austin changed from a nearly all-white to a nearly all-black neighborhood during the decade.

Table 2.1. Racial change in UHD neighborhoods 1970 to 1980

City/community	% Black 1970	% Black 1980	% Change
Atlanta			
Oakland City	47	93	46
Baltimore			
Park Heights	77	94	17
Chicago			
Austin	2	94	92
Roseland	36	97	61
Cincinnati			
Madisonville	33	69	36
Columbus			
Near South Side	55	66	11
Dallas			
Trinity-Lisbon	53	78	25
Decatur (Georgia)			
South Decatur	62	72	10
Freeport (New York)	37	55	18
Gary			
Horace Mann	31	60	29
Indianapolis			
Forest Manor	85	96	11
Brookside	2	7	5

City/community	% Black 1970	% Black 1980	% Change
Islip			
Old Central Islip	8	16	8
Jersey City			
Greenville	37	69	32
Kansas City			
Blue Hills	18	71	53
49–63 Area	55	89	34
Milwaukee			
Eastside	15	25	10
Northwest Side	53	80	27
Westside	4	21	17
Minneapolis			
Northside	22	36	14
New York City			
South Ozone Park	59	77	18
Baisley Park	92	96	4
Brighton	16	26	10
Oakland			
San Antonio	47	61	14
Fruitvale	13	31	18
Central E. Oakland	53	74	21
Elmhurst #1	70	86	16
Elmhurst #2	55	78	23
Elmnurst #3	39	75	36
Elmhurst #4	87	91	4
Philadelphia			
Wynnefield	64	84	20
East Mt. Airy	64	87	23
Rockford			
Westside	23	41	18
South Bend			
Riverside Manor	0	15	15
Rum Village	11	20	9
La Salle Park	33	45	12

City/community	% Black 1970	% Black 1980	% Change
Tacoma			
Census tract 613	8	11	3
Census tract 617	60	50	-10
Census tract 621	17	20	3
Wilmington			
Baynard Boulevard	85	92	7
Price's Run	28	58	30
Westside	47	49	2

The results were obtained by first weighting the census data to take into account the proportion of the tract in the UHD neighborhood and by next aggregating the results from the tracts for the UHD neighborhoods. The following example from Decatur (1970) illustrates the technique.

1. Weight the tract based on the proportion of the tract in the UHD

Census tract	% Black	(% of tract in UHD neighborhood)
227	77	100
228	33	50

2. Multiply the weighting factor by the raw proportion and sum, the resulting product

$$77 \times 100 = 7700$$
$$33 \times 50 = \underline{1650}$$

3. Calculate the weighted mean by dividing the product by the weighting factor, i.e., $9250/150 = 62\%$.

Most cities had insufficient time to plan and implement new neighborhood preservation programs in conjunction with homesteading. Consequently, most expanded programs that were already in operation. These included (1) housing maintenance programs (code enforcement, rehabilitation loans and grants, home repair), (2) physical improvement programs (streets, parks and recreation), and (3) municipal services (e.g., enhanced police patrols, special refuse collections).

Despite the dramatic racial shifts that were occurring, none of the cities implemented programs explicitly aimed at racial stabilization. This may reflect the mistaken belief that socio-economic/racial stabilization is not a necessary part of neighborhood preservation efforts (USR&E, 1978, p. 70). Further-more, the noninvolvement reflects the low priority that central city governments have assigned to racial stabilization efforts.[5]

b. PROPERTIES. In selecting properties for the homesteading program, cities tried to screen out "rehab liabilities" (too expen-sive to rehabilitate) and those that were in such good condition as to constitute a "giveaway." One way that cities eliminated "rehab liabilities" and "giveaways" was to specify maximum and minimum rehabilitation costs (e.g., more than $10,000, less than $1,500).

As of April 1979, 2,273 properties were transferred from HUD to cities. Not surprisingly, the vast majority (96 percent) were single family residences (USR&E, 1979). Of the 2,273, three-fourths (73 percent) were occupied by homesteaders, and one-half were fully rehabilitated. Over the course of the Demonstration, the value of the properties transferred from HUD to the cities in-creased, reflecting greater selectivity on the part of local homesteading agencies.

c. HOMESTEADERS. Of the approximately 50,000 households who applied for the homesteading program as of April 1979, 2,101 or 4 percent were selected. Homesteaders tended to be young (average age 35.7), middle-income (average income $17,000 in 1979, just below the national average of $17,730), and black (about two-thirds). The overwhelming majority had previously been renters prior to the program. Thus, the homesteading agen-cies succeeded in selecting householders who were in need, yet capable of making improvements.

Most cities used a lottery to select homesteaders as equitably as possible. The typical approach, used in thirteen of the twenty-three programs, was first to screen applicants for suitability and match them with a property and then to use the lottery to assign homesteaders for each property. Five selection criteria were employed: (1) demographic (e.g., families were usually given priority over individuals); (2) previous housing tenure and/or housing need (most cities gave preference to renters, the level of overcrowding being one of the housing need criteria); (3) financial capability (minimum/maximum income limits, indebtedness, credit rating); (4) self-help skills (ability to do some of the rehabilitation work); and (5) social behavior and attitudes (e.g., membership in a civic association, character, housekeeping habits).

2. Benefits of the Program

Homesteading families realized substantial benefits in the form of increased housing quality with only a modest increase in the monthly cost of the housing (USR&E, 1983, p. 6). Most of the homesteaders were able to obtain far better housing than in the rental units they previously occupied. The homesteader's principal "consumption" benefit was the writedown in property costs. "The homesteaders receive the unrepaired property at no cost to them, so that after repair many of them have received an asset for substantially less than the market value" (p. 58). Homesteaders received two other "consumption benefits" in addition to the writedown: subsidized mortgages (either from the 312 program or from a municipal program), and property tax exemptions and abatements.

Homesteaders also benefited from the appreciation in value of the property over and above the rehabilitation costs. Together, the aggregate net benefits after three-year occupancy, assuming sale of property (consumption benefits and appreciation in value), totaled $11,500.

USR&E (1983, p. 7) also asserted that the Demonstration was successful in upgrading neighborhood housing conditions and in achieving socioeconomic stabilization, but, as we shall see, the evidence does not support this assertion. Resident survey data did indicate that the rate of racial change slowed down during the period of the Demonstration (1977–1979) from what it had been earlier during the 1970s. Similarly, after declining during the early 1970s, median income levels rose during the Demonstration period at the same rate as the national population. Further, during the last part of the 1970s, home investment levels rose more rapidly than nationally. Finally, compared with control neighborhoods, property values "were no longer losing ground after 1977, [p. 7]" whereas they had been dropping behind during the 1970 to 1977 period.

A closer inspection of the results, however, questions the asserted cause-effect relation between Urban Homesteading and revitalization. First, the decline in the rate of racial transition during the late 1970s may simply reflect the racial turnover of many of the UHD neighborhoods by this point in time (see Table 2.1) and the fact that the proportion of blacks could not rise further. Furthermore, the rapid outmigration of white owners continued, and this was precisely the group that the program sought to retain. That these communities were able to retain white renters is not a great achievement. Transitional communities typically retain disproportionate numbers of renters because they do not have to make the type of long-term commitment to the area that owners do.

Second, the criteria for judging revitalization success was probably too lenient. One could argue that, given the large federal and local expenditures involved, the Demonstration should have sought to reduce the gap between UHD neighborhoods and others, rather than simply to "slow the rate of decline."

Third, any improvements in neighborhood conditions during this period may have been due to macroeconomic factors rather than the UHD. The late 1970s were a period of high interest rates. Skyrocketing housing costs (a macro factor) made older homes in central city communities attractive to families of modest means. Middle-income families may have remained in, and been attracted to, the UHD neighborhoods because of housing market conditions rather than any components of the program.

Fourth, encouraging results may reflect the aggregation of survey results from forty highly diverse neighborhoods. It is conceivable that improvements in a few large, predominantly white neighborhoods counterbalanced declines in many other small, racially changing, ones. USR&E failed to examine differences in rates of improvement between different community types, and as a result, it is impossible to test for the validity of this explanation. This issue will be addressed in later chapters.

Finally, it is difficult to reconcile USR&E's positive assessment of the program in terms of neighborhood impacts with the mixed and inconclusive results from the windshield and residents surveys. While there was a significant increase between 1977 and 1979 in the proportion of dwelling units with exterior paint in good condition, there were significant declines in the proportion of roads, curbs and sidewalks in good condition. Similarly, while there were significant drops in the proportion of neighborhood residents bothered by crime, there were significant increases in the proportions bothered by specific environmental problems: street noise, dangerous traffic, bad roads and run-down houses.

Perhaps the weak *overall* neighborhood impacts should not be surprising, given the low density of homesteading activity and the short duration of the Demonstration. However, even on homesteading blocks, evidence of "spillovers" is negligible and contradictory. Therefore, USR&E's conclusion that the program did promote revitalization (USR&E, 1983, p. 7), is unconvincing.

The consultant notes that over the course of the Demonstration there was a reduction in the gap, in social and physical conditions, between blocks immediately surrounding homesteaders (proximity category I) and blocks further away (proximity categories II and III). At the beginning of the Demonstration, the blocks in proximity zone I had the lowest income levels and were most poorly maintained. By the end of the Demonstration, the gap had closed largely due to improvements in homesteading blocks. USR&E speculated that homesteading activity attracted middle-income families and spurred existing residents to make home improvements.

It is equally plausible, however, that these improvements were due to intraneighborhood differences in mobility patterns that had nothing to do with the Demonstration. Mobility rates were highest on homesteading blocks and declined as distance from homesteading properties increased. The high rates of turnover provided the opportunities for middle-income families to move into these sections, thereby explaining the rise in income levels. These families undoubtedly pressured city agencies to improve physical conditions, to fix streets, to remove refuse, and so forth.

USR&E acknowledges another finding contradicting the existence of "spillovers." Investment rates were highest at the start of the Demonstration in areas close to homesteading properties reflecting the high rate of physical deterioration on these blocks but *during* the Demonstration rose most rapidly in proximity zone II.

The fact that investment rates were lowest in the areas close to urban homesteads by 1979 seems to suggest that the conjec-

tured spillover effects of the program in terms of inducing nearby homeowners to maintain and improve their properties do
not exist. (USR&E, 1983, p. 94).

Later chapters, which include more sophisticated statistical tests
of the impact of proximity to homesteading, reaffirm the same
negative results.

Conclusion

How can one explain the negligible neighborhood impacts of
the UHD both at the block and neighborhood levels? It is likely
that the short time span of the Demonstration and the low density
of homesteading activity partially explain this finding. In addition,
the narrow scope of the program (homesteading plus supportive
services primarily aimed at physical housing problems) prevented
it from influencing the dramatic racial and race-related shifts occurring in many of the UHD communities.

If neighborhood preservation programs are to be made more
effective, they will have to encompass programs focused directly
on racial and socioeconomic stabilization. In order to develop
such programs, better information is needed on the impact of
racial and socioeconomic shifts on the mobility and home improvement decisions of both white and black families.[6] This book
aims to make a contribution in this area.

Chapter *3*

Urban Homesteading and Socioeconomic Stabilization

When the federal government's Urban Homesteading Demonstration began in late 1975, it was expected to stabilize the populations in the neighborhoods surrounding homesteading properties, thereby slowing decline and facilitating the upgrading of housing conditions. An evaluation of the UHD by USR&E (1983, p. 7) concluded that the Demonstration was achieving the desired stabilization. That is, during the 1977 to 1979 period, racial turnover slowed, and the income and educational levels of owners rose, implying that the UHD did have the desired effect.

However, as noted earlier, this conclusion is suspect for two reasons. First, there were no control neighborhoods. The same types of improvements may have occurred in similar neighborhoods without homesteading. Second, the aggregate results might mask important differences in the impact of the program between cities with different housing markets (e.g., tight markets with low vacancy rates versus loose markets with high vacancy rates). Because USR&E's research was completed before the 1980 census, it was not possible to examine 1970 to 1980 shifts in these neighborhoods.

This chapter does examine the socioeconomic changes in the UHD neighborhoods between 1970 and 1980 and compares them with the changes in control neighborhoods within the same cities, areas similar with respect to socioeconomic characteristics but which did not have Urban Homesteading. It is hypothesized that UHD neighborhoods would experience greater increases in median income level, in the proportion of owners, and in the proportion of whites (three frequently utilized measures of neighborhood improvement).[1] The improvement of the UHD neighborhoods relative to the controls would reflect the impact of homesteading activity. That is, the rehabilitation of previously vacant homes would make neighboring residents more confident about their neighborhood, making them more likely to remain and inducing middle-income residents to relocate into the community who otherwise would not consider doing so. We assume, however, that neighborhood conservation programs implemented in conjunction with homesteading were *equally or more important* in affecting population shifts.

Our tests of these hypotheses should be considered tentative since the program had only been in operation for two to three years at the time of the 1980 census. This may have been too short a time period for the program to have any meaningful neighborhood impacts. Second, since census data is gathered every ten years, it is of limited value for tracking community change. For example, it is possible that the UHD neighborhoods experienced declines in the early part of the decade and rebounded in the second part, but it is impossible to detect these shifts with data available only for 1970 and 1980. Third, the census tracts may be too large and diverse to detect improvement. Improvements on homesteading blocks may have been counterbalanced by declines elsewhere in the census tract. Due to this problem, Lee & Mergenhagen (1984) and Zais & Thibodeau (1983) failed to detect gentrification in a number of communities widely perceived to be undergoing this process. It follows that it would be even harder to detect rises in socioeconomic levels stemming from neighborhood conservation programs, since the expected changes are much smaller. Despite these weaknesses, the census is by far the most convenient and accurate data source for assessing neighborhood change across a number of cities.

Furthermore, the statistical procedure used for "matching" demonstration and nondemonstration neighborhoods may not have paired truly comparable neighborhoods. The procedure insures a match on selected demographic characteristics of the population but not on such variables as residential density, nature of the housing stock, physical layout, character of public services, and so on. This fact could severely limit comparability. While our results are not likely to be fully conclusive, they should help in assessing existing claims regarding the stabilizing effects of Urban Homesteading.

This chapter adds to the limited number of census analyses of neighborhood conservation programs. Ahlbrandt & Brophy (1975) and McFarland (1984) have used census data to examine the impacts of the NHS model and the Community Development Block Grant (CDBG) program, respectively. However, both studies identified the control neighborhoods impressionistically. In contrast, this chapter uses a more objective statistical approach to specify control neighborhoods and applies it to several key cities in the United States.

Methods

A computer tape containing 1970 and 1980 census tract information for U.S. cities was used to identify control neighborhoods for the forty-five UHD communities.[2] A tract that fell within one standard deviation from the range for the UHD tracts for three 1970 variables (percent minority [black and Hispanic], median family income, and percent owners) was chosen as a control tract. A two-tailed t-test was used to compare the homesteading tracts, as a group, with the control tracts.

It was impossible to identify a sufficient number of control tracts in fifteen of the UHD cities, and consequently the chapter focuses on the remaining eight.

Findings

There are few consistent patterns between the UHD and control neighborhoods (Table 3.1). Both the UHD neighborhoods and the control tracts experienced declines in their standing on median income level relative to their SMSAs. In relative terms, the

Dallas and Philadelphia UHDs experienced improvement versus the control tracts, though the opposite was true for Chicago and Milwaukee.

Even though the UHD neighborhoods attracted both white and black homesteaders, the program appears to have had little or no impact on racial transition in the surrounding areas. All of the UHD neighborhoods either were predominantly black in 1970 or experienced a large increase in the proportion of blacks during the 1970s. In the three cities where both the UHD neighborhoods and the control tracts were racially mixed in 1970 (i.e., less than 50 percent black: Baltimore, Boston, Milwaukee), the rate of racial turnover was greater in the UHD tracts.

Finally, there was little evidence that the program had any effect on the conversion of buildings from rental to owner occupancy. With the exception of the control tracts in Dallas, there were only miniscule percentage changes in owner occupancy. Where there were meaningful shifts, the direction of the results varies. The Philadelphia UHD neighborhood experienced the most clear-cut improvement, an increase in owner occupancy. This was in sharp contrast to the decline occurring in the control tracts. In contrast, the Milwaukee UHDs experienced more rapid declines in owner occupancy than in the control areas.

Conclusions

Proponents of housing conservation programs are bound to be disappointed by the absence of neighborhood impacts from Urban Homesteading. The hope, or fear, among some that homesteading would lead to gentrification was exaggerated. Homesteading neighborhoods were no more likely to experience increases in income levels or conversions from renter to owner occupancy than were the control tracts.

Two pieces of evidence imply that homesteading was not even effective in stabilizing the populations in these areas. Many of the UHD neighborhoods fell behind the control tracts with respect to shifts in income levels and owner occupancy. Furthermore, although it is impossible to determine whether homesteading sped up the process of racial change in some way, the UHD neighborhoods experienced more rapid racial turnover than the control tracts.

Let us now look at one neighborhood in detail over time to better understand racial and race-related shifts which impeded neighborhood upgrading efforts.

Table 3.1. Comparisons of homesteading and control census tracts (Nonhomesteading/Homesteading)

	No. of Tracts	1970 Income Ratio	Change Income Ratio	1970 Percent Minority	Change Percent Minority	1970 Percent Owner	Change Percent Owner
Atlanta	5	76.20	-18.80	0.51	0.36	0.48	- .05
	2	76.50	-18.50	0.53	0.39	0.58	- .02
Baltimore	33	75.73	-14.57	0.85	0.04	0.36	0.02
	5	76.28	-19.07	0.78	0.17	0.34	0.03
Boston	23	77.52	-15.52	0.05	0.12[a]	0.29	-0.02
	5	77.40	-19.27	0.15	0.42	0.29	-0.02
Chicago	238	89.02	-10.04[b]	0.11	0.29[b]	0.37	0.01
	5	90.00	-28.80	0.18	0.79	0.36	0.00
Dallas	2	85.18	-26.72	0.67	0.24	0.56	-0.11
	3	84.67	-11.00	0.79	0.12	0.77	-0.03
Milwaukee	140	87.37	- 7.75[b]	0.11	0.11[b]	0.47	-0.01[b]
	42	76.40	-19.31	0.43	0.20	0.34	-0.03
New York	113	100.07	- 1.43	0.67	0.15[b]	0.65	-0.05
	23	90.61	- 6.13	0.90	0.05	0.68	-0.03
Philadelphia	51	83.02	-16.61[b]	0.66	0.19	0.67	-0.05
	6	107.83	- 7.17	0.67	0.21	0.67	0.02

Notes
   a. Significant at .05 level.
   b. Significant at .01 level.

The analysis for this table utilized census data from 45 UHD neighborhoods in 23 cities; the 40 original neighborhoods plus 5 additional ones added at the time of the wave 2 survey. The remainder of this book uses survey data from the original 40 UHD neighborhoods.

Chapter 4

Wynnefield: A Racially Changing UHD Community

If it is true that racial change is an obstacle to neighborhood upgrading efforts (Clay, 1979), then the Urban Homesteading Demonstration would have had limited prospects for success, since so many of the UHD communities experienced racial turnover during the 1960s and 1970s. This chapter examines the impact of racial shifts on socioeconomic levels and on community institutions and standards through a case study of Wynnefield, one of two racially changing UHD communities in Philadelphia.[1] Wynnefield is typical of the UHD communities that experienced racial transition (see Varady and Torok, 1984); therefore, the results of this chapter should be generalizable to many of the other UHD communities.

Wynnefield is a roughly two and one-half square mile area in West Philadelphia containing about 20,000 people. The community's boundaries consist of the city limits to the north (City Line Avenue), a large park (Fairmount Park) to the east, railroad tracks to the south, and another residential community (Overbrook Park) to the west.

Wynnefield is divided into two sections on the basis of housing type and density. The northern half of the community, Upper Wynnefield, has a relatively low density and is characterized by single family homes on large half-acre lots. The remainder of the community, Lower Wynnefield, is typified by single family row

57

houses with some duplexes and triplexes. Lower Wynnefield more closely resembles inner-city sections of Philadelphia, while Upper Wynnefield resembles nearby sections of Lower Merion Township.

The Wynnefield UHD comprises most of Lower Wynnefield (70 percent of one tract and 95 percent of another), as well as a tiny part of Upper Wynnefield (10 percent of one tract). For practical purposes the UHD can be considered equivalent to Lower Wynnefield.

Early history

Wynnefield was first settled in 1690 by Dr. Thomas Wynne, a colonial physician. During the eighteenth and nineteenth centuries, prosperous Protestant families purchased attractive detached houses on large plots of land in the Upper Hill section of the community, closest to the city boundary. Development accelerated in the 1920s, as block after block in Lower Wynnefield was subdivided and developed for attached and semiattached homes. Most of these were purchased by Eastern European Jewish immigrants relocating from South Philadelphia, the city's equivalent of New York City's Lower East Side. More affluent Jews moved to the Upper Hill section of the community. As the number of Jews increased, Protestant families moved away. By 1930, Wynnefield had all of the characteristics of a second generation Jewish ghetto, with communal life centered around the many congregations located in the community.

Although Wynnefield retained its Jewish character from the end of World War II until the mid 1960s, it was becoming increasingly susceptible to racial change. Discriminatory housing practices against Jews began to disappear, and more affluent Jewish families were able to relocate to Philadelphia's prestigious Main Line suburbs. When the children of Wynnefield families married, they sought homes in newer sections of the metropolitan area rather than near their parents in Wynnefield. Finally, during the 1950s and 1960s, the boundaries of West Philadelphia's black ghetto shifted outward toward Wynnefield. By 1960, sections of West Philadelphia immediately adjacent to Wynnefield were predominantly black.

The 1960s: Wynnefield undergoes racial transition

In 1963, the first black family moved into a home in Lower Wynnefield that had been made available by the Federal Housing Administration as the result of a foreclosure. The succeeding black families first tended to cluster in Lower Wynnefield but later purchased homes throughout the community.

The inmigration of blacks led to the fear among established white residents that the community would undergo rapid racial change and that community standards would decline. The Jewish Community Relations Council (JCRC) of Philadelphia undertook research to ease these fears. Property transfers were studied to determine the rate of racial change; community workers were interviewed to determine the impact of racial changes on community standards. In its final report, the JCRC concluded that ". . . racial changes taking place in the area are not drastic, have not depreciated property values, quality of public education and have not in any way impaired the neighborhood" (Jewish Community Relations Council of Greater Philadelphia, undated, p. 10). This evaluation was overly optimistic in light of later events.

As has been the case in other racially changing middle-class communities, the main mechanism for achieving stable integration was the local civic association, the Wynnefield Residents Association (WRA). The programs of the WRA were typical of those of civic associations in other racially changing communities in that they focused on the overall quality of life for all residents rather than on racial stabilization per se (organization block clubs, lobbying for improved city services and facilities, and so on).

These stabilization efforts were not successful. During the late 1960s there was a sharp drop in the number of whites purchasing homes in Lower Wynnefield and a correspondingly sharp increase in the number of blacks purchasing. Racial transition was not attributable solely to a drop in white demand; black inmigration contributed to an acceleration of white outmigration. These "panic moves" were due to the perception of living in a predominantly black neighborhood (combined with an unwillingness to be part of a racial minority), along with a concern about violent street crime (Varady, 1979).

Between 1960 and 1970 Wynnefield changed from predominantly white to demographically biracial (51 percent black). The rate of racial change was even greater in Lower Wynnefield (later selected as the UHD neighborhood) which was 70 percent black by 1970. The slow rate of racial change in Upper Wynnefield (85 percent white in 1970) was due more to the attractive housing values than to the programs of the WRA.

In Wynnefield, as in other racially changing communities, turnover involved the replacement of middle-aged and elderly whites by younger black families. As of 1970, the median age was eighteen years higher for whites than blacks (43 as compared to 25). Furthermore, as has been the case elsewhere, racial change during the 1960s was not associated with declines in income or educational levels.

Racial succession was, however, associated with a number of community problems, of which crime was the most serious. During the early 1970s, the community was shocked by a series of muggings and stabbings of middle-aged and elderly women. Later, teenage gang violence became a problem. Police statistics also provide an indication of the severity of the problem. Murder, rape, robbery and aggravated assault were far more common in Wynnefield in 1973 than in adjoining Lower Merion Township, even though the population of Wynnefield was only one-third of the latter area. Furthermore, total crime, which includes less serious crimes in addition to the ones listed above, rose more rapidly in the 19th Police District (which encompasses Wynnefield and other sections of West Philadelphia), than in Lower Merion Township. White residents were particularly likely to view crime as a problem because they were likely to compare the incidence of crime to the period prior to racial change (when it was a rarity).

It is difficult to account for the rise in crime, since a middle-income black population replaced a middle-income white one. One possibility, based on the experience of the South Shore Community in Chicago, is that, as the racial composition of the community shifted, Wynnefield was increasingly perceived by inner-city black residents as part of the "ghetto." Outsiders may have committed much of the crime occurring in the community. Unfortunately, data are lacking to support this assertion. The rising street crime problem could also reflect the increase in the number of families with both spouses working. Lack of parental supervision would enable teenagers to become involved in gangs, drugs and other forms of criminality.

In common with other racially changing communities, racial shifts in the public schools occurred more rapidly than in the surrounding community. Many of the remaining whites were middle-aged or elderly couples who no longer had children at home. In addition, many of the whites with school-aged children sent them to private or parochial schools or to one of the two "elite" Philadelphia public high schools drawing students from the city as a whole. Overbrook High School, serving Wynnefield and other areas of West Philadelphia, had a black majority as early as 1961. The junior high school and two elementary schools began to change in 1964, and, by 1973, all four schools were at least 85 percent black. Falling test scores and overcrowding were additional problems.

Racial change had an enormous impact on the Jewish institutions in the community. Three congregations closed their doors and relocated during the late 1960s. A fourth Reform congregation remained and attempted to promote interracial harmony by making its facility available to a black Baptist congregation and later by opening a bicultural nursery school for black and Jewish children. In 1983, it too decided to relocate. All of these congregational decisions were made with little fanfare and on the basis of impressionistic evidence related to community change. In contrast, Har Zion Temple, a large Conservative congregation decided to relocate in 1973 after sponsoring an intensive community survey (see Klausner and Varady, 1970, and Varady, forthcoming) and while under the scrutiny of national as well as local media. The relocation may have had a shattering impact on the already low morale of remaining Jewish residents, whether they attended services or not, because the closing symbolized the demise of the Jewish community.

Wynnefield is one of the areas where racial change lowered property values. During the 1960s, the mean property value declined by 17 percent, from $13,118 to $10,916, taking into account the effects of inflation. During this period, property values rose by 7 percent in Lower Merion Township. Those selling large single family homes in Upper Wynnefield had a particularly difficult time finding buyers and often sold for one-half or one-third the cost of similar homes in nearby Lower Merion.

Vacant homes were another serious community problem. The Office of Finance of the City of Philadelphia defined a vacant home as one that had been unoccupied for at least a year, regardless of its physical condition or marketability. As of Spring 1974, there were a total of 114 vacant homes in the community. Although there were vacant units spread throughout the entire community, vacant homes were concentrated in one part of Lower Wynnefield. The existence of this concentration was one reason why Wynnefield was designated an Urban Homesteading Demonstration neighborhood.

Philadelphia's homesteading program had actually preceded the federal Demonstration, with the City Council authorizing a program in 1973.[2] The Philadelphia Housing and Development Corporation was chosen to supervise the conveyance process.

East Mt. Airy, another older racially changing neighborhood, was chosen for the Demonstration along with Wynnefield. The existence of strong resident associations, along with a high proportion of homeowners and an attractive housing stock, were important in selecting these two areas.

> Active community groups in both areas have played a key role in *successfully stabilizing their neighborhoods*, having their areas designated for the homesteading Demonstration, and subsequently serving as a communications network to publicize program and coordinate supportive neighborhood conservation activities. (Emphasis added, USR&E, 1977, vol. 3, p. 143).

Although the term "stabilization" is not defined in this report, few impartial observers would consider Wynnefield an example of a stable community, given the rapid racial change, the depressed housing prices, and the problem of street crime. Further, there is no reason to believe that the activities of the WRA lessened the severity of these problems.

This is not intended as a criticism of the WRA, since all three of these problems had causes that were metropolitan or societal in nature, and it would be unrealistic to expect a civic association to solve them. The fact that the term "stabilization" was not defined is probably not coincidental but, rather, reflected an unwillingness on the part of the city of Philadelphia, HUD and USR&E to confront directly the subjects of race and racial change.

Philadelphia is one of the few UHD cities not to use a lottery system for selecting homesteaders. An initial screening process eliminated the majority of applicants. The Homesteader Board made the final selection from among those that were eligible. In order to increase the Demonstration's likelihood of success, Philadelphia utilized the best available vacant dwellings.

Philadelphia's program is one of those emphasizing the use of contractors, rather than self-help. Rehabilitation counselors did, however, encourage homesteaders to do limited carpentry and painting. An Urban Homesteading revolving loan fund, financed by a city bond issue, was used to provide interim loans to participants to enable them to begin rehabilitation. Once rehabilitation began, the city helped homesteaders secure permanent mortgages from private banks. Thirteen banks developed a special mortgage plan, "The Philadelphia Plan," to meet mortgage needs. The most unique feature of the plan was that the income of a borrower's spouse or of a co-mortgagee was recognized as effective income, as was income from a welfare agency.

Neighborhood conservation programs in Wynnefield and Mt. Airy were limited in magnitude and scope. Two hundred thousand dollars in Community Development Block Grant funds were made available for small physical improvements in these communities, but, as of 1977, only a small portion had been used for tree trim and a paint program. The latter set up a voucher system for paint and brushes to enable residents to paint their houses.

Specific information is unavailable on the status of homesteading properties in each of Philadelphia's two UHD neighborhoods, and we must therefore rely on aggregated information for the two (USR&E, 1978). As of April 1978, 232 properties had been transferred from HUD to the city of Philadelphia, 102 homesteaders had been selected and 89 properties transferred from the city to homesteaders. With respect to the latter 89 properties, rehabilitation had started in 82, the properties occupied numbered 72, and rehabilitation completed in 63. Thus, assuming that there were similar numbers of homesteading properties in Mt. Airy and Wynnefield, the overall incidence of homesteading was low, relative to the total housing stock of the two areas. Further, assuming homesteading properties were clustered within the two communities, the impact of the rehabilitation on the surrounding communities would probably be limited.

The 1970s and 1980s: Wynnefield as a middle income black community

Newspaper articles about Wynnefield during the late 1960s and throughout the 1970s reflected the hopes and beliefs of Wynnefield residents that stable racial integration could be achieved. This optimism is reflected in two newspaper headlines: "Wynnefield is a Neighborhood that is 'Making It' " (*Jewish Exponent*, 1969), and "Integration Success: Wynnefield Survives, Prospers as a Community in which Races Exist Together" (Lee, 1979). A small surge in home purchases by young whites during the early 1970s further encouraged optimism. However, the outmigration of whites continued during the 1970s. Although data is lacking on whether the outmigration resulted from panic moving or normal turnover, the result was the same. Most of the homes put up for sale were purchased by blacks. Visions of a stable integrated community dissipated as Wynnefield was perceived as a middle-income black area.

By 1980 Wynnefield was 74 percent black. Lower Wynnefield was overwhelmingly (93 percent) black, while in Upper Wynnefield whites were still in the majority (65 percent). However, these figures greatly exaggerate the amount of demographic integration in Upper Wynnefield, since a disproportionately large number of the whites (50 percent versus 22 percent for blacks) were in nonfamily units (i.e., students at St. Joseph's College and long term patients in the Home for Incurables). Furthermore, a large proportion of the remaining white population lived in Wynnefield Heights, physically separated from the rest of the community by a golf course.

Differences between whites and blacks in demographic characteristics widened during the 1970s because white outmigration was selective from among younger and more affluent families. Whereas 34 percent of the white population was elderly, this was only true for 8 percent of the black population. Similarly, while the most common household type among whites was a husband/wife unit without children (60 percent), the "norm" (40 percent) for blacks was a husband/wife unit with children.

The outmigration of affluent whites during the 70s also altered the white-black comparison on income level. In 1970, the median income of whites ($11,371) was 10 percent higher than for blacks ($10,354). By 1980, the median black income level ($19,698) was 5 percent higher than for whites ($18,648). Educational levels were virtually identical (12.2 years for whites and 12.1 for blacks).

Racial shifts during the 1970s did not adversely affect the socioeconomic complexion of the population *as a whole*. During the 1970s the median income level rose by two-thirds, 67 percent, from $11,499 to $19,249. (These figures are not adjusted for changes in the cost of living.) There was virtually no change in the occupational makeup of the population during this period, with 29 percent at both points in time employed in "prestigious" occupations (professionals and managers).

The preceding figures showing socioeconomic stability (or improvement) mask a growng lower income population in Lower Wynnefield (the UHD neighborhood). During the 1970s, the proportion below the poverty line doubled from 8.8 to 15.6 percent, and the proportion dependent on public assistance rose from 3 to 21 percent. There was also evidence of increased family disorganization and breakup, with a doubling of female-headed households (16 to 30 percent) and a corresponding decrease in the percentage of children living with both parents from 75 to 61 percent. This pattern of overall economic stability with a growing lower income population was characteristic of other UHD neighborhoods as well (Varady and Torok, 1984).

Housing prices continued to be depressed during the 1970s, with values decreasing from $14,325 to $12,690, adjusted for declines in the value of the dollar, whereas values rose by 5 percent during this period for the city as a whole. Wynnefield experienced a 3 percent increase in overcrowding for the community as a whole (from 3 to 6 percent). It is unknown whether this increase led to a worsening of housing conditions, since increased density does not necessarily lead to greater "wear and tear."

Supplementing the objective data presented thus far, the UHD longitudinal neighborhood residents survey data set describes residents' *assessments* of housing and neighborhood conditions as of 1977. As shown in Table 4.1, UHD residents generally were satisfied with their housing conditions, with four-fitths of the Wynnefield residents and three-fourths of the residents elsewhere rating their housing as good. UHD residents (Wynnefield and elsewhere) tended to rate their neighborhoods as worse than their homes. However, Wynnefield residents felt more positively about neighborhood conditions than respondents in other communities. This is shown by the smaller proportion of Wynnefield residents that rated their neighborhood as bad or "so-so" and the higher proportion of Wynnefield residents that perceived no neighborhood physical problems (litter, traffic, and so on). There was, however, one exception to this generalization: Wynnefield residents were more likely to be aware of and concerned about abandoned housing.

Given the seriousness of street crime in Wynnefield during the 1970s, the survey results are surprising. A large majority of the Wynnefield residents, like residents in the other UHD neighborhoods, did *not* see crime as a serious problem and were satisfied with police protection. The nature of the crime problem seems to have been different in Wynnefield from elsewhere. Whereas Wynnefield residents were significantly more likely to be concerned about drugs, they were significantly less likely to have been burglarized.

The relatively low level of concern about neighborhood crime and the high level of satisfaction with police protection among Wynnefield respondents may seem surprising to the reader, since objectively street crime *was* a serious problem in the community in the 1970s. It should be noted, however, that most of the Wynnefield respondents to the UHD study were black, and it is likely that most of them had moved from inner-city areas where crime and other neighborhood problems were considerably worse. Their positive evaluations were due, therefore, as much to their earlier migration history as to the objective conditions involved.[3]

The outmigration of the white/Jewish population was accompanied by a decreased Jewish institutional presence. Of the eight congregations that had been in the community in 1965, only four (three Orthodox and one Conservative) remained in 1984. All four Jewish day schools which had been in Wynnefield had relocated. One Jewish institution, the Talmudic Yeshiva was thriving, however, with 200 live-in students from the East Coast and Canada. Although the Yeshiva has remained aloof from integration efforts, it has expanded its physical facility and encouraged Orthodox families to purchase in the area. These efforts may succeed in maintaining a viable Jewish enclave in one small part of Upper Wynnefield.

Conclusion

This case study verifies much of what is already known about racially changing middle-class communities. First, racial change involved both pull and push factors. That, is the decline in the white population was due to the attraction of existing and prospective residents to newer suburban areas, as well as to a reluctance to remaining in an area where whites were a cultural and racial minority. Second, as elsewhere, racial change had more of an impact on community institutions and community standards (e.g., crime) than on the socioeconomic characteristics of the population. Finally, the Wynnefield Residents Association was just as ineffective in arresting racial transition as other civic associations have been in other racially changing communities.

It is impossible to say whether racial change was "good" or "bad." From a Jewish perspective, change was problematic because of the high costs of institutional relocation and because many white residents suffered as a result of having to relocate from a familiar environment. On the other hand, from a black perspective, racial change was beneficial because it enabled many middle and working-class black families to improve their housing and neighborhood conditions. Although many of the black families undoubtedly would have preferred Wynnefield to remain integrated, the continued turnover probably was not viewed that seriously, since their primary objective was achieving an improved quality of life.

It is possible that the benefits to blacks were only temporary. Racial change was accompanied by a number of community problems—street crime, depressed housing prices, a growing lower income population—which threatened the stability of the area as a middle-income community. It is possible that these problems made black homeowners pessimistic about the future of their area, making them unwilling to remain and improve their properties. Later chapters test for these behavioral impacts.

The UHD was supposed to have helped to stabilize the population. In order to do so, it would have had to reassure homeowners about the above three problems, as well as others. However, the Demonstration (at least in this community) seemed incapable of doing this. The written materials reviewed suggest that program planners were unwilling or unable to formulate clearly defined objectives related to population stabilization. In addition, homesteading activity was probably too limited to have a significant impact on the surrounding community. Finally, the neighborhood conservation programs administered in conjunction with the UHD not only were underfunded but inadequately focused on population stabilization.

Table 4.1* Comparison of Wynnefield and non-Wynnefield residents on housing and neighborhood assessments

Characteristic	Other UHD (n = 1707**)	Wynnefield (n = 47**)	Significance
Overall housing condition Good	74%	80%	n.s.
General neighborhood rating Bad to so-so	62	47	.05
Number of neighborhood physical problems None	32	43	n.s.
Abandoned homes Not concerned	71	55	.03

Characteristic	Other UHD (n = 1707**)	Wynnefield (n = 47**)	Significance
Crime a Problem			
No	67	68	n.s.
Drugs a problem			
Somewhat or big			
problem	32	63	.00001
Whether burglarized			
No	78	96	.006
Satisfaction with			
public services			
Satisfied with all	37	45	n.s.
Whether satisfied			
with police			
Satisfied	75	77	n.s.

Notes:

*In order to save space, this table presents an abbreviated version of the bivariate crosstabular results. The full results can be obtained from the figures shown. For example, the first set of figures should be read as follows. Of the approximately 1700 non-Wynnefield respondents, 74 percent rated their home as good, while the remainder rated it as so-so or poor. Of the 47 Wynnefield respondents, 80 percent rated it as good and 20 as so-so or bad.

**The actual sample sizes vary somewhat for the separate analyses listed below.

Chapter *5*

Neighborhood Confidence

Chapter 3 showed that Urban Homesteading Demonstration neighborhoods were not more likely than controls to experience socioeconomic improvements. This finding alone is *not* conclusive evidence of the ineffectiveness of homesteading as an upgrading strategy. It is possible that the program improved housing and social conditions but only on blocks immediately surrounding homesteading properties. A more definitive assessment of homesteading requires examining the influence of homesteading activity on nearby residents. Fortunately, the longitudinal UHD neighborhood residents data set facilitates such an evaluation by providing information on the distance of the respondent from the nearest homesteading property (i.e., same block, two or three blocks away, four or more blocks away). The next three chapters test whether proximity to homesteading made nonparticipating residents more confident about their neighborhood's future, thereby making them more likely to remain and invest in their properties. This chapter focuses on the impact of homesteading on confidence levels.

More specifically, the chapter seeks to answer two sets of questions. First, what was the impact of homesteading activity on confidence levels over the two year Demonstration period, as compared to other personal and neighborhood characteristics? Respondents living close to a homesteading property were expected to be more aware of upgrading activity than others living further away,[1] making them more confident about their neighborhood's future. Second, how did different characteristics

71

affect confidence levels? Which characteristics had an indirect effect on confidence by first affecting particular neighborhood
assessments (perceived neighborhood environmental problems),
and which characteristics had a direct effect on confidence? For
example, low-income families might be pessimistic, regardless of
their evaluations of neighborhood conditions, due to their own
financial situation.

The definition of neighborhood confidence used in this book is
drawn from Goetze (1979, p. 92):

> . . . the conviction on the part of residents and others in touch
> with the neighborhood that change will not come at a rate or in
> ways that prevent . . . social norms from controlling events.

For the sake of clarity and simplicity, we operationally define
neighborhood confidence as positive expectations related to the
future and pessimism as negative expectations.

Relation to previous research

Although there is consensus among social scientists about the
importance of neighborhood confidence in these decisions
(Downs, 1981; Goetze, 1976, p. 129–130), there has been virtually
no empirical research on this attitude (Galster and Hesser, 1982).
Hollister's evaluation of Boston's Neighborhood Confidence Project (1978), mentioned in Chapter One, probably the most detailed
study thus far, has serious methodological flaws. Hollister concep-
tualized confidence as consisting of past, present and future components. Specific measures included moving plans, expectations
of what the neighborhood would be like in three years, recent
trends in property values, and whether the respondent would
recommend the neighborhood to a friend. Neighborhoods were
ranked based on the results to the four questions; neighborhood
confidence scores were obtained by adding the individual rank-
ings. Aggregate analysis related neighborhood confidence levels
to particular population characteristics (e.g., the proportion of
owners).

The most serious flaw in the study was the measure of confidence. In contrast to other authors who stress that confidence is

related to the future (Goetze, 1979), Hollister gave equal weight to past, present and future. His own results showed that past and present attitudes were not correlated with future feelings. His respondents, who had positive feelings about the neighborhood's past and present, but who were concerned about the future, could hardly be considered optimistic. The neighborhood confidence measure used in this book is more consistent with the research literature because it stresses expectations. Second, Hollister's aggregate type analysis illustrates the ecological fallacy whereby it is erroneous to particularize from groups to individuals.

Although there has been little empirical research on the determinants of neighborhood confidence, there has been considerable speculation on the underlying causes. Scholars have disagreed on the importance of four different types of factors. One group asserts the importance of concerns about ethnic and income shifts as a cause of pessimism and decline; ethnic homogeneity has been linked to confidence. Goetze (1979) notes that stereotyping and prejudice may affect the reactions to black newcomers. The concerns may become self-fulfilling prophesies. On the other hand, Downs (1981) stresses that some of the fears of whites are realistic. Racial change is often followed by socioeconomic decline, reflecting the difficulty of middle-class black families in separating themselves spatially from lower class families.

Others have stressed the importance of physical conditions in affecting neighborhood change. For example, most theories of neighborhood decline are based on the concepts of housing filtration or appraisers' beliefs about housing age, condition, and obsolescence going hand-in-hand (Goetze, 1980, p. 16). These theories imply that declines in the physical condition of housing and neighborhoods are the prime determinants of neighborhood pessimism.

A third group has emphasized the importance of the neighborhood social fabric in affecting neighborhood confidence. A strong social fabric is often reflected in the existence of a residents' association which is able to lobby effectively for public services. However, the social fabric may be revealed in informal ways, as well. In strong socially cohesive neighborhoods, social pressure by neighbors leads to conformance to local norms regarding home maintenance (Galster and Hesser, 1982). Ahlbrandt and Cunningham found that the neighborhood social fabric influenced neighborhood commitment; this strongly implies that the social fabric would influence confidence levels, as well.

Finally, many authors have stressed the importance of the quality of public services in affecting confidence levels (Ahlbrandt and Brophy, 1979; Ahlbrandt and Cunningham, 1974; Goetze, 1976). Grigsby et al. (1977) emphasizes that in order to promote socioeconomic and racial stability in revitalizing neighborhoods, it is important to pay more attention to the quality of local public schools.

This chapter builds upon the earlier, mostly speculative research by testing for the importance of these four different types of neighborhood concerns. It also adds to the limited social science literature on the geographic or spatial aspects of the neighborhood spillovers phenomenon (the indirect benefits or harms from housing programs that are limited to the immediate area). To date, most research on neighborhood effects has focused on the extent of impact (e.g., property value increases) in association with particular housing programs. There has been little research on the behavioral processes underlying this phenomena: that is, how the improvements influence attitudes which, in turn, affect behavior. By examining the link between homesteading activity and confidence levels, this chapter should help to narrow this gap.

This research goes considerably beyond earlier analyses of the UHD, completed by Urban Systems, Research and Engineering, Inc. Pedone, Remch and Case, (1980) found "that the overall attitudes of UHD residents toward their neighborhoods did not vary significantly between 1977 and 1979." For example, over the two-year period, residents' ratings of their neighborhoods on a scale of 1 to 5 (bad to good) remained virtually unchanged, decreasing slightly from 3.4 to 3.3 (Pedone, Remch and Case, 1980, p. 95). This implies that the Demonstration did not raise confidence levels. But such a conclusion may not be warranted, due to the analytic approach used: a comparison of the overall results for the sample as a whole for 1977 and 1979. No adjustment was made for migration flows during the period. Those who remained during the course of the Demonstration may have become more confident, but this trend could have been obscured by the inclusion of new families. Furthermore, the seemingly stable results seen could mask considerable shifting at the household level. The lack of change could simply reflect the fact that the numbers becoming optimistic were balanced by the numbers becoming pessimistic. This chapter responds to the need to know not only how much shifting occurred but also the underlying causes of this shifting. Assuming that homesteading activity did lead to higher confidence levels, was this because the program improved vacant and blighted structures, because it led to improved public services, or because it promoted middle-class migration to the area? The analysis which follows should help to answer these questions.

This chapter builds upon the Pedone study in a second way by incorporating 1980 and 1970 census data into the analysis, whereas Pedone relied exclusively on 1970 data. Using census data for both periods permits us to examine how objective in-

Figure 5.1 **Neighborhood Confidence Model**

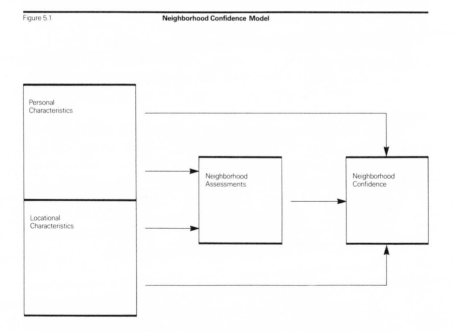

dicators of neighborhood change influence confidence, as well as how the composition at one point in time influences this attitude.

Existing research provides little guidance as to whether the adverse effects of upgrading on confidence levels of certain groups outweigh the beneficial effects on others. That is, low-income families and the elderly may fear that they will be displaced as a result of rising rents and rising property values. To date, there has been little research on whether this belief about the adverse effects of upgrading is realistic or exaggerated.

Figure 5.1, the conceptual model for this chapter, is a modified version of a model of environmental satisfaction developed by Marans and Rogers (1972). According to the model, neighborhood confidence is dependent on an individual's assessments of different aspects of the environment (e.g., demographic shifts, public services). These assessments are influenced by objective neighborhood conditions and personal characteristics which include all aspects and experiences of individuals that might influence their perceptions and evaluations.

Methods

This and the following three chapters utilize the longitudinal Urban Homesteading Demonstration neighborhood residents data set consisting of three waves of approximately 1700 interviews during the 1977 to 1979 period. The survey was described in greater detail in Chapter 2.

Neighborhood confidence was measured by an index formed from two questions, one dealing with expected changes in the neighborhood and the second with the current neighborhood rating. Respondents were first asked:

Thinking about what this neighborhood will be like in three years or so, do you expect it to be: a better place to live, a worse place to live, or about the same as now?

They were later asked:

In this last question about your neighborhood, I'd like you to look at this scale from one to five. One would be extremely bad, and five would be extremely good. How would you rate your neighborhood, overall, on this scale?

Comparable neighborhood confidence indices were formed for 1977 and 1979 by crosstabulating the neighborhood expectation and neighborhood ratings variables. (See Table 5.1 for the 1977 results.) Respondents were considered "confident" if they expected their neighborhood to get better regardless of its current conditions, or if they expected the neighborhood to remain the same, and they rated it very good. Conversely the "pessimists" were those who expected their neighborhood to get worse regardless of its current condition, or who expected the neighborhood to remain the same and rated it as very bad. A middle group, neither optimistic nor pessimistic expected their neighborhood to remain the same and rated it "so-so."

As of 1977, less than one-half (45 percent) of the respondents were confident about their neighborhood's future. One-fourth (25 percent) were pessimistic, while about one-third (30 percent) were neither pessimistic nor optimistic. Over the next two years, confidence levels remained relatively stable, with *the sample as a whole* becoming slightly more optimistic. In 1979, 50 percent were optimistic, 24 percent were pessimistic, and 26 percent were neither.

The overall stability for the sample as a whole is deceptive and masks considerable shifting among individual householders. A crosstabulation of the 1977 and 1979 confidence measures for the 650 households that remained over the two-year period indicates one-half (50 percent) changed their opinion about the neighborhood's future, while the remainder maintained their same assessment.

Multiple regression analysis is used to explain variations in the incidence of different neighborhood-related concerns (e.g., racial change) in 1979 and in the likelihood of being confident about the neighborhood's future at that point in time.[2] The analytic strategy is to examine the influence of different background characteristics from 1977 (including neighborhood attitudes at that point in time) on both neighborhood concerns and neighborhood confidence in 1979. The regressions were run in two stages. We first tested for the determinants of different neighborhood-related concerns. Next, the determinants of neighborhood confidence were examined, including both 1979 neighborhood concerns and other background characteristics. The regressions were run for the 273 households who remained over the two-year period and for whom complete information was available on all of the variables in the confidence model.[3]

Table 5.2 summarizes the preliminary regression results for the sample as a whole and for the white and black subsamples. The regressions were rerun, including only those that were significant at the .05 level. The final regression results are represented by a path diagram (Figure 5.2). The hypothesized causal relationships are represented by unidirectional arrows extending from each determining variable to each variable dependent upon it. Residual variables are represented by other unidirectional arrows leading from the residual variable to the dependent variable. Standardized regression coefficients are placed on the unidirectional arrows and provide evidence of the relative importance of the independent variables.

Table 5.3 summarizes the information in the path diagrams by indicating the indirect, direct, and total effects of the different variables. In order to measure the indirect effects, it was necessary to compute the effects of the background characteristics through the different paths portrayed in Figure 5.2 (e.g., poor housing conditions to concern about abandoned homes to neighborhood pessimism). This was done by multiplying the separate betas (i.e., using the above example, -.27 X -.11 = .03). The results from the separate indirect paths were added to compute the total indirect effects. The total effect for each variable was obtained by adding the direct and indirect effects.

Findings

In contrast to what was expected, homesteading activity did not raise confidence levels. Proximity to homesteading properties had a slight indirect negative impact on confidence. This almost insignificant finding masks two counterbalancing results (Figure 5.2). On the one hand, living on a homesteading block contributed to optimism through a lack of concern about income change. The inmigration of middle-income black and white families as homesteaders apparently made residents on homesteading blocks feel more positively about population shifts than those living further away.

On the other hand, this positive impact of homesteading was more than counterbalanced by the stronger indirect impact of proximity on pessimism through a concern about abandoned properties. At the beginning of the Demonstration, the homesteading blocks had the highest incidence of vacant properties and physical decay. After the two-year Demonstration was over, the remaining vacant properties bothered nearby residents. It is possible, although impossible to confirm, that the Demonstration made nearby residents more sensitive to the vacant properties that remained.

Although homesteading activity did not affect confidence in the UHD neighborhoods as a whole, it is possible that it did have an impact in particular types of communities. Clay's assertion (1979) that racial change is an obstacle to successful neighborhood upgrading implies that homesteading activity would have a greater impact in areas experiencing little racial change. This hypothesis was not supported by a separate regression run (results not presented here) limited to respondents in neighborhoods experiencing relatively little change, an increase of 18 percent or less between 1970 and 1980. In this regression run, the proximity variable played the same insignificant role that it did in the run for neighborhoods experiencing rapid racial change.

Confidence levels were shaped by respondents' evaluations of demographic shifts that were occurring in the UHD areas in the mid and late 1970s. The 1979 neighborhood evaluations which included concerns about racial and income changes explained an additional 23 percent of the variance in neighborhood confidence beyond what was explained by background personal and neighborhood characteristics (Table 5.4). Worries about income changes played a more important explanatory role than worries about racial change. Whereas the concern about income change was one of the most important predictors of pessimism (beta = .17, Figure 5.2), the concern about racial change did not have a statistically significant impact.[4] There was, however, some limited evidence that racial changes did have an impact on confidence levels. Living in a neighborhood that experienced a large increase in the proportion of blacks during the 1970s directly contributed to neighborhood pessimism, while being a white in a predominantly white neighborhood promoted confidence.[5]

Were concerns about income change self-fulfilling prophecies

Figure 5.2   **Path diagram, determinants of
                              neighborhood confidence (1979).
                              Standardized regression coefficients.
                              (Part I)**

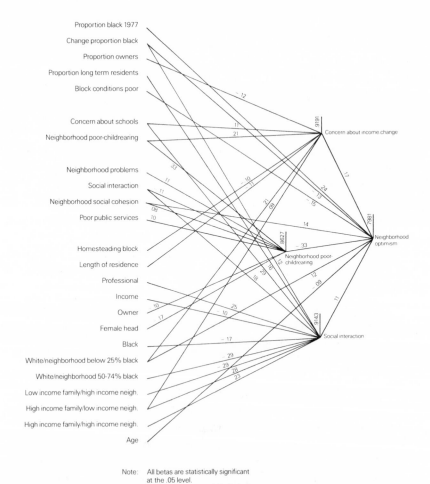

Note: All betas are statistically significant
        at the .05 level.
        Background characteristics include
        neighborhood assessments from 1977.

by whites stemming from racial stereotypes? Or were these concerns perhaps shared by blacks as well, suggesting that they resulted from realistic assessments of what was occurring in the surrounding areas? The findings support the second interpretation. Although whites were somewhat more likely than blacks to be concerned about income changes (27 percent, 205, versus 16 percent, 374, p < .004), a substantial number of blacks were concerned. Furthermore, the concern about income change was a

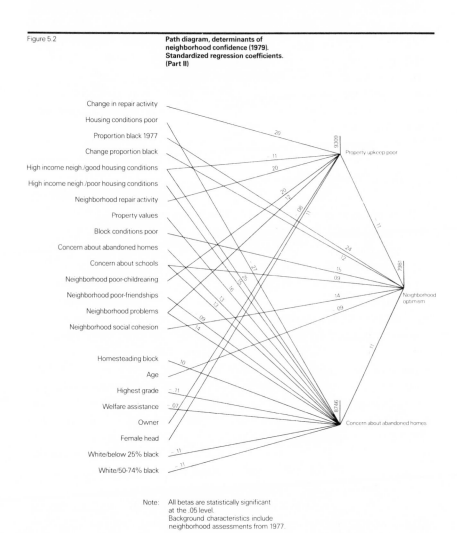

Figure 5.2

Path diagram, determinants of
neighborhood confidence (1979).
Standardized regression coefficients.
(Part II)

Note: All betas are statistically significant
at the .05 level.
Background characteristics include
neighborhood assessments from 1977.

more important predictor of pessimism among blacks than whites.

Worry over socioeconomic changes reflected shifts that were actually occurring in the UHD communities. The average respondent lived in a neighborhood experiencing a 20 percent increase in the proportion of blacks during the 1970s. Similarly, the concern about socioeconomic decline had some basis in reality (Varady and Torok, 1984). While increases in the mean income levels of the UHD neighborhoods generally resembled those of the cities in which they were located, many of the UHD neighborhoods during this period experienced disproportionately large increases in female-headed households and welfare families. The growing lower class/lower income presence probably disturbed many middle class families, both black and white, who believed that a continuation of this pattern would undermine their dominant position in the neighborhood. Thus, the concerns about income change were not simply a result of racial and class stereotyping, but reflected accurate assessments of what was occurring in these areas.[6]

Concerns about the adequacy of the neighborhood for childrearing were even more important than fears related to demographic shifts in influencing householders' attitudes toward the neighborhood's future. Childrearing adequacy was the most important predictor of neighborhood pessimism. Contrary to what might be expected, this neighborhood assessment was not a function of the quality of the local public schools. The 1977 evaluation of the local public schools had little, if any, impact on the neighborhood rating for childrearing. Instead, this rating appears to have been based on perceived changes in the extent to which middle-class values were dominant in the area. Middle-class parents seek neighborhoods where their values are the dominant ones and where their children meet others from similar backgrounds. Middle-class parents of both races might have feared that, with the growing presence of lower class households, there would be an increased likelihood of their children becoming involved in gangs and/or drugs, or that it would be dangerous for their children to walk unescorted in the neighborhood.

It is surprising that this variable was equally important among whites and blacks even though whites were far less likely to have school age children (41 percent, 224 versus 66 percent, 417, p < .000). Whites may have been concerned about the inadequacy of the neighborhood for childrearing, fearing that this weakness would deter other whites from moving into the area.

Two other measures of the quality of the social fabric proved to be unimportant in the analysis: the cohesiveness of the neighborhood (the friendliness of neighbors, the ease in identifying strangers), and the rating of the neighborhood for making adult friends. The insignificance of the neighborhood rating for adult friendships reflects the ability of parents to attract friends from a large area, whereas their children depend on the immediate block and neighborhood. Thus, the UHD neighborhoods seem to have had more difficulty holding and attracting middle-income families with children than those without.

As expected, the level of neighborhood social cohesiveness played an important explanatory role, as did the respondent's level of social interaction in the surrounding neighborhood. Those who met frequently with neighbors and who knew most or all of them well enough to talk to them were far more likely to be confident about the neighborhood's future than those with weak local ties. It is likely that strong neighborhood social patterns led to a loyalty to the area that inspired confidence about its future.

Although concerns about demographic changes and about the quality of the social fabric played a key role in affecting confidence, physical conditions did have an influence. Living in a neighborhood with inadequately maintained streets, sidewalks and curbs (as measured on the windshield survey) directly contributed to pessimism. In addition, a concern about abandoned properties contributed to pessimism. However, more is involved in the latter result than simply worry about physical blight. Parents may have been concerned about abandoned homes because the dwellings constituted attractive but dangerous play areas for children and could be used as gang hideouts. The latter interpretation is supported by a strong bivariate correlation (.19) between a poor neighborhood rating for childrearing and a concern about abandoned housing and the fact that black households, which were more likely to have children, were more likely to be worried by abandoned dwellings.[7]

The results in Figure 5.2 refute previous thinking about the influence of public services on confidence levels. An index measuring dissatisfaction with one or more public services played no explanatory role. While it is true that public school-oriented parents who were dissatisfied with local public schools were particularly likely to be pessimistic,[8] only 7 percent of the sample had this combination of characteristics. Attempts to raise confidence levels among existing residents by improving the public schools could only have a limited potential for success because of the small size of the group that could be affected. Such efforts may, however, be more important in attracting middle-class public school-oriented families to the area.

A 1980 report by Pedone, Remch, and Case indicates that the UHD stimulated widespread repair activity. Previous writings on residential displacement in revitalizing neighborhoods (U.S. Department of Housing and Urban Development, 1981) imply that this activity would inspire fear among low income families, female-headed households, the elderly, and so forth that rising rents could lead to forced moves. Figure 5.2 provides conflicting evidence in relation to this hypothesis. The fact that the elderly were particularly likely to be pessimistic about their neighborhood's future seems to support the displacement argument. This finding could, however, reflect the personal situation of these householders. The elderly may have been pessimistic because of declining health or other factors unrelated to the Demonstration. In order to determine which explanation was more valid, displacement or personal situation, we redid the regression analysis on the portion of the sample living in neighborhoods with a high level of repair activity. The fact that age did not play an especially important role suggests that the second explanation is more likely to be true. That is, the results (not presented here) reflect the precarious health and financial situation of the elderly rather than any adverse effects of the Demonstration.[9]

The results for female-headed households contradict the displacement thesis in that this type of household was more optimistic than others about the neighborhood's future. This finding resulted from female household heads rating their neighborhoods high for childrearing and being less concerned about abandoned homes. This finding may reflect lower standards and expectations among these women because they moved from inner-city neighborhoods where conditions were considerably worse.

Conclusion

This has been one of the first empirical analyses of the determinants of neighborhood confidence in inner-city areas. Stepwise regression analysis was applied to the longitudinal UHD neighborhood residents data set to determine the importance of homesteading relative to other personal and neighborhood characteristics in explaining levels of confidence at the end of the Demonstration (1979).

Homesteading activity did have a small positive effect on confidence levels of residents on homesteading streets by reassuring them about population shifts. This small positive effect was more than counterbalanced by a pessimism based on the continued presence of abandoned properties on these streets. Thus, the Demonstration did not live up to the hopes of housing advocates that it would raise confidence levels. Confidence levels were influenced by demographic shifts, which had a shattering effect on the social fabric, and, to a lesser extent, by physical declines occurring in these communities. Concerns about income shifts and abandoned homes, as well as low neighborhood ratings for childrearing and property upkeep, were particularly important in promoting pessimism. The UHD was incapable of addressing these concerns because of the small proportion of homesteading properties in particular communities and the lack of programs dealing specifically with population shifts. Residents of cohesive neighborhoods and those who interacted frequently with neighbors tended to be most confident about the area's future. The policy implications of this finding are uncertain, however, because local governments possess limited tools to create such socially integrated areas.

Finally, there was no evidence that revitalization had any adverse effects on the confidence levels of needy subgroups, such as low-income renters, long-term elderly residents and welfare recipients. Thus, the results support neither the exaggerated hopes for homesteading nor the exaggerated fears of its impacts through displacement.

Table 5.1. Neighborhood confidence variable, 1977: expected changes in three years by current neighborhood rating (Percentage in cell out of total)

| | Neighborhood rating, 1977 | | |
Expected changes	Relatively Bad	So-so	Relatively Good
Better	1%	8%	10%
	(1)	(1)	(1)
Same	4	30	26
	(3)	(2)	(1)
Worse	7	11	3
	(3)	(3)	(3)

Note: Numbers in parentheses refer to the following confidence categories:
(1) optimistic,
(2) neither optimistic nor pessimistic,
(3) pessimistic.

Table 5.2. Regression results, determinants of neighborhood confidence. Total sample, whites, blacks (Standardized regression coefficients)

Characteristic	Total sample	Whites	Blacks
Neighborhood poor for childrearing, 1979	-.31[a]	-.34[a]	-.39[a]
Concern about income change, 1979	-.20[a]	-.14	-.19[a]
Cohesive neighborhood, 1977	.14[a]	.04[a]	.14[a]
Proportion of long-term residents	.07	.41[a]	.00
Poor property maintenance, 1979	-.08[a]	-.21[a]	.02
Concern about housing abandonment, 1979	-.13[a]	.08	-.18[a]

Characteristic	Total sample	Whites	Blacks
Poor property maintenance, 1977	.07	-.09	.13[a]
Owner	.08	-.19[a]	-.12
Social interaction, 1979	.11[a]	.14	.01
Neighborhood proportion black	.32[a]	.76	.25[a]
Poor block conditions	-.19[a]	-.21[a]	-.12
White/neigh. under 25% black	.20[a]	.37	—
Age	-.09[a]	-.34[a]	.07
Concern about schools, 1977	-.08[a]	-.15[a]	.05
Change in neigh. property repair expenditures	.15[a]	.48[a]	.03
Neighborhood poor for friendships, 1977	-.06	.17	[b]
Neighborhood social cohesiveness, 1979	.07	.20	.00
Concern about schools, 1979	.05	.08	.05
White/neigh. 25 to 49% black	.09	.25	—
Neighborhood repair activity, 1979	-.19[a]	-.86[a]	-.03
Change in neighborhood prop., black	-.14[a]	.03	-.26
Property values	-.16	-.15	-.18[a]
Low income neigh./poor housing conditions	.00	-.50[a]	.49[a]
Concern about racial change, 1979	.06	-.05	.11
Concern about income change, 1977	-.04	-.05	-.08

Characteristic	Total sample	Whites	Blacks
Proportion of old buildings	-.06	-.19	-.03
White/neigh. 50–74% black	.07	.11	—
Neighborhood problems 1979	-.05	-.10	.05
Neighborhood poor for friendships, 1979	.03	.08	-.04
High income neigh./good housing conditions	.14	-.26	.40[a]
High income neigh./poor housing conditions	.12	-.38	.45[a]
High family/high neighborhood income	-.11	-.47	.14
Low family/high neighborhood income	-.05	-.15	-.03
Change in neigh. property values	-.03	-.06	-.07
Female household head	-.02	-.09	-.05
High family/low neighborhood income	-.02	-.03	.10
Length of residence	-.02	.11	.01
Social interaction, 1977	.02	.07	[b]
Poor neighborhood housing conditions	-.04	-.05	-.24
Professional worker	-.01	-.17	.07
Concern about housing abandonment, 1977	.01	.10	-.05
Welfare assistance	-.01	-.08	.05
Employed	-.01	-.13	-.04
Neighborhood environmental problems, 1977	-.01	-.01	.04
Income	[b]	-.21	-.07

Characteristic	Total sample	Whites	Blacks
Highest grade	b	.31	-.04
Unskilled worker	b	.01	.04
School aged children	b	.07	-.03
White/neigh. 75% or more black	b	b	—
Concern about racial change, 1977	b	.15	.07
Same block as homesteading block	b	-.24[a]	.04
Df	278	93	185
R2	.41	.76	.49

Notes
a. Statistically significant at the .05 level.
b. Variable not included because it did not meet statistical significance and/or tolerance criteria.

See Appendix Table 1 for definitions of the above variables.

Table 5.3. Indirect, direct and total effects of background and intermediary variables on neighborhood optimism

Characteristic	Indirect effects	Direct effects	Total effects
Housing conditions	.03	.00	.03
Proportion black	.00	.24	.24
Change neighborhood proportion black	.01	-.13	-.12
Block conditions poor	.00	-.15	-.15
Neighborhood proportion owners	.03	.00	.03
Proportion of long-time residents	.02	.00	.02

Characteristic	Indirect effects	Direct effects	Total effects
High neighborhood income/ good housing condition	-.02	.00	-.02
High neighborhood income/ poor housing condition	-.02	.00	-.02
Neighborhood repair expenditures	-.02	.00	-.02
Change in repair expenditures	-.02	.00	-.02
Property values	-.02	.00	-.02
Concern about schools, 1977	.00	-.09	-.09
Neighborhood poor for childrearing, 1977	-.17	.00	-.17
Neighborhood poor for friendships, 1977	.01	.00	.01
Neighborhood problems, 1977	-.07	.00	-.07
Social interaction, 1977	.02	.00	.02
Socially cohesive neighborhood, 1977	.03	.14	.17
Poor public services	-.03	.00	-.03
Same block as homesteading property	-.01	.00	-.01
Age	.00	-.09	-.09
Highest grade	.01	.00	.01
Professional	.03	.00	.03
Welfare assistance	.01	.00	.01
Owner	.04	.00	.04
Female household head	.07	.00	.07

Characteristic	Indirect effects	Direct effects	Total effects
White/neighborhood under 25% black	-.01	.12	.11
White/neighborhood 50–74% black	.01	.00	.01
Black	-.03	.00	-.03
Low family income/ high neighborhood income	.01	.00	.01
High family income/ high neighborhood income	.03	.00	.03
High family income/low neighborhood income	.03	.00	.03
Length of residence	.01	.00	.01
Concern about income change, 1979	—	-.17	-.17
Neighborhood poor for childrearing, 1979	—	-.33	-.33
Property upkeep poor, 1979	—	-.11	-.11
Social interaction, 1979	—	.11	.11
Concern about abandoned homes, 1979	—	-.11	-.11

Table 5.4. Total and partial R2s of background characteristics on neighborhood optimism

Variable set	Total R2	Partial R2
Demographic characteristics	.0297	.0297[a]
1977 neighborhood attitudes (over and beyond demographic characteristics	.1680	.1432
Objective neighborhood characteristics (over and beyond demographic charactistics and 1977 attitudes)	.2343	.0797
1979 neighborhood attitudes (over and beyond demographic characteristics 1977 neighborhood attitudes and objective neighborhood characteristics)	.4112	.2337

Note

a. Calculated as follows: $\frac{R2\ with - R2\ without}{1 - R2\ without}$ where R2 with is the fraction of variance in pessimism explained by the predictor variable group plus all prior prediction groups, and R2 without is the fraction of variance in pessimism explained by all prior predictor variables.

Chapter 6

Residential Mobility

If revitalization programs like the Urban Homesteading Demonstration are to succeed, they must stabilize the neighborhood populations; that is, they must hold and attract middle-income families (Ahlbrandt and Cunningham 1979; Goetze, 1976; Grigsby et al., 1977; Public Affairs Counseling, 1975). This chapter evaluates the effect of the UHD on mobility decisions of nonparticipating neighbors and tests whether the Demonstration helped to hold middle-income families and white ones. It also examines the importance of the household's proximity to a homesteading property in affecting those decisions, beyond other background personal, housing, and locational characteristics. It was hypothesized that people living on a block with a homesteading property would be more likely to be aware of the program's existence than would residents elsewhere in the neighborhood. Enhanced awareness would give them greater optimism about the neighborhood's future than other residents had, making them more likely to stay. Other hypotheses also are tested.

This chapter utilizes a mobility model developed and tested by MacMillan (1980) which is a refined version of one created by Speare, Goldstein, and Frey (1974).[1] The model assumes that the mobility process consists of four stages: dissatisfaction, plans to move, the search, and the move itself. The model presumes that a certain level of dissatisfaction is necessary before a household will consider moving.[2] However, the relation between stages is not perfect. Some people are forced to move, even though they are satisfied, or move because they find a better opportunity. Other families remain, despite this dissatisfaction, because of an unwillingness to incur the psychological and monetary costs of relocating. Our model builds upon MacMillan's by adding neighborhood confidence as an intermediary variable between background characteristics and mobility.

The model predicts that background characteristics influence mobility in three ways: by affecting the level of satisfaction with the home or the level of confidence in the neighborhood, by affecting the threshold at which dissatisfaction or pessimism is translated into plans or plans into behavior, and by influencing the ability to carry out a search for a new home.

Figure 6.1 **Mobility Model**

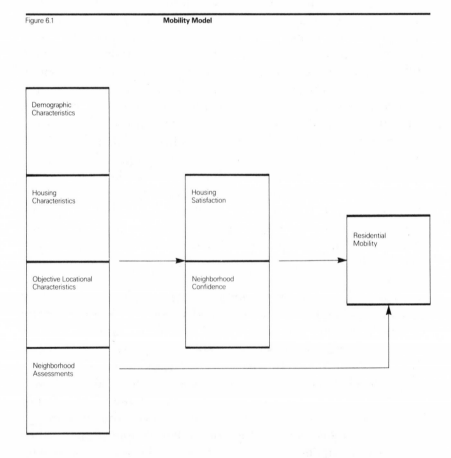

This chapter uses a simplified version of MacMillan's model (Figure 6.1) which includes only three sets of variables: background personal characteristics and residential problems, housing satisfaction and neighborhood confidence, and mobility behavior. It is hypothesized that the background characteristics and problems can affect mobility in either a direct or an indirect manner. For example, owning could promote residential stability through higher levels of housing satisfaction. It could also lead to staying through the high transaction costs of moving for owners.

This chapter makes three specific contributions to the neighborhood revitalization literature. It is one of the first to test for the impact of a government housing program on residential mobility. Other examples of this type of research include: R. Ginsberg, 1983; MacMillan, 1980; Pedone, 1982; and Pedone, Remch and Case, 1980. In contrast to Ahlbrandt and Cunningham's Pittsburgh study (1979) which used people's plans to move as a measure of mobility behavior, this chapter examines actual mobility behavior in various neighborhoods throughout the country. Second, this is one of the first empirical tests of the importance of neighborhood confidence (residents' optimism or pessimism about the future quality of the neighborhood) in affecting the moving decisions of people in inner-city communities. Goetze (1976) and others have only asserted that this factor is important. Finally, this chapter goes considerably beyond two earlier works on what determines people's decisions about moving in the UHD neighborhoods (Schnare, 1979; Pedone, Remch and Case, 1980) in examining the role of racial and socioeconomic changes that affect these decisions.

Methods

This chapter, like the preceding one, consists of secondary analysis of data from the longitudinal Urban Homesteading Demonstration neighborhood residents surveys. The analytic strategy is to test for the impact of background characteristics, housing satisfaction, and neighborhood confidence (all measured in 1977) on mobility behavior over the course of the Demonstration (i.e., whether the household remained at the location in the neighborhood less than one year, between one and two years, or two years or more). Stepwise multiple regression is used to examine the importance of different background characteristics in explaining variations in neighborhood confidence,[3] housing satisfaction, and mobility behavior. In the first set of runs, every independent variable was included that was hypothesized to be important, based on the mobility model. These results are presented in Table 6.1. The regressions were then rerun, excluding variables that were statistically insignificant at the .05 level or that did not meet the tolerance level of .01. The results are shown in a path diagram (Figure 6.2). Separate regressions were run for low-income families (below $12,000) and higher income ones ($12,000 and higher); as well as for white and black families. There were few meaningful differences between the two racial and the two income groups, and, consequently, separate path diagrams were not prepared for these subgroups. Table 6.2 summarizes the path model by showing the indirect, direct and total effects of the different independent variables.

Findings

Contrary to expectations, the results provide no evidence that proximity to homesteading activity had any effect on neighbors' decisions about moving; nor was there support for the belief that the program would have a disproportionately greater effect on middle-income families. Families who lived on a block containing a homesteading property were not more likely to stay than other families. As shown in Table 6.1, the proximity variable failed to meet tolerance or significance criteria and consequently, was not included in the regression equation. Nor was there any evidence that homesteading was more influential in affecting mobility decisions in racially homogenous communities as compared to those undergoing racial transition. In a separate regression run, results not presented here, limited to neighborhoods experiencing little racial change during the 1970s, the proximity variable played as small an explanatory role as it did in the analysis for the sample as a whole.

These results may indicate that the number of homesteading

dwellings in any one neighborhood was too low to influence neighbors' confidence in the neighborhood. Unfortunately, the UHD data did not include a measure of the density of homesteading activity on the block; consequently, it was not possible to test whether the Demonstration had a greater effect on decisions about moving in neighborhoods where there was relatively more homesteading.

Alternatively, the Demonstration may have had little impact because the homesteading properties were on blocks that had the highest incidence of physical deterioration. Improvements by homesteaders may not have been great enough to alter the overall image of decay in these areas. This speculation is supported by statistically significant correlations at the .001 level between living on a block with homesteading properties and the level of deterioration of both properties and street conditions measured by the windshield surveys (.10 and .13 respectively).

There was no support for the frequently made assertion that the quality of public services, and, in particular, the quality of local public schools, plays an influential role in decisions on whether to move away from inner-city areas (Ahlbrandt and Brophy, 1975; Ahlbrandt and Cunningham, 1979; Grigsby et al., 1977; Orfield, 1981). Nor was there evidence that these factors were consequential in affecting middle-income householders' decisions about moving. There was an insignificant correlation among confidence in the neighborhood's future, satisfaction with housing, and moving, on the one hand, and a Likert-type scale measuring the number of perceived problems with public services, on the other. In addition, householders who valued high-quality public schools and who had doubts about their neighborhood's public school were no more likely to move than others were. This latter finding may seem surprising and counterintuitive, particularly in light of the consensus among many economists and others that public service quality does influence migration decisions. It should be noted, however, that this chapter's findings are consistent with most other empirical research on the subject. Further, it is likely that these evaluations play a significant role in affecting *where* householders choose to move rather than *when* they decide to move. Additional research is warranted on the first type of migration decision.

Similarly, the general quality of the neighborhood had little impact on migration decisions. In fact, two of the indicators of the health and viability of the neighborhood (mean property values and mean property investment levels in the neighborhood) increased the likelihood that residents would move away rather than stay (Figure 6.2).

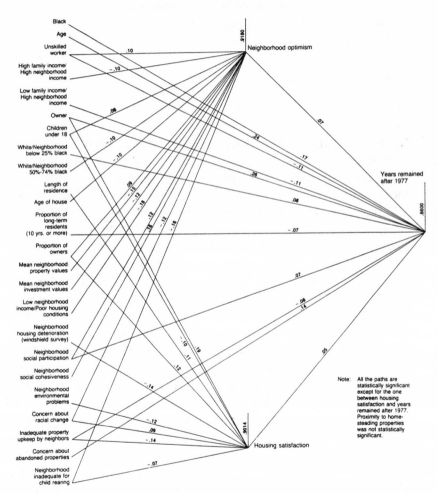

Figure 6.2 **Path diagram of factors affecting residential mobility (i.e., amount of time remained at residence after 1977 interview)**

The results support previous research showing racial change playing a role in explaining neighborhood decline (Goetze, 1976; Public Affairs Counseling, 1975). Concerns about racial change contributed to residents' decisions to move away by increasing pessimism about the neighborhood's future. Furthermore, whites in a community with a black majority (50 to 74 percent in 1977) were highly likely to move, while those in predominantly white communities (less than 25 percent black) were especially unlikely to move.

Concerns about the quality of the area for childrearing were particularly important in explaining outmigration. The belief that the area was not good for childrearing encouraged people to move away, by increasing their dissatisfaction with their housing, as well as their pessimism about the neighborhood's future. Whites with children may have been uncomfortable about having their children become part of a racial minority which might lead to problems of socialization and peer group relations (Downs, 1968). This concern was not limited to whites, however, as indicated by the moderate (.09) correlation between race (being white) and this rating. As noted earlier, middle-class blacks may have been worried about the arrival of lower income black families and possible increases in crime, drug use, and so forth. Concerns about forming adult friendships, however, did not play an influential role in the analysis, presumably because adults could draw their friends from a wide area.

Recent empirical research suggests that residents of socially cohesive nighborhoods are more likely to feel optimistic about the future of the neighborhood than are residents of less cohesive neighborhoods (Ahlbrandt and Cunningham, 1979). Although the results are mixed, they tend to support that conclusion. Respondents who said they lived in neighborhoods where neighbors were friendly, and where it was easy to identify strangers, tended to be confident about the neighborhood's future and were less likely to move. Similarly, residents of neighborhoods with a high proportion of homeowners (an indicator of a cohesive neighborhood) also tended to be optimistic about the neighborhood's future and also were satisfied with their housing conditions. Surprisingly, those who lived in a neighborhood with a high proportion of long-term residents were more likely to move than to stay.

There was support for the hypothesis that social integration into the surrounding neighborhood contributes to residents' attachment to the area (Ahlbrandt and Cunningham, 1979; Galster and Hesser, 1982). Those who socialized frequently with neighbors on the block and who knew neighbors well enough to stop and talk with them were confident about the area's future, and that promoted residential stability. This variable also directly increased the likelihood of staying.

Three of the findings support the assertion that physical deterioration of buildings, as well as socioeconomic changes, contributes to neighborhood decline. First, the perception that neighbors did not take adequate care of their property had direct and indirect effects on people's decisions about moving. The overall effect of this variable (Table 6.2) was far greater than that of the other two measures of environmental problems. This finding highlights the importance of the social cohesiveness of the neighborhood in influencing mobility decisions, since high levels of upkeep signify closely knit areas (Schoenberg and Rosenbaum, 1980). Second, the perception that the neighborhood had a relatively large number of environmental problems (such as street noise; dangerous street traffic; streets or roads in need of repair; inadequate street lighting; trash, litter or junk in the street; people living in houses that were run down; and neighborhood crime) encouraged people to move away by increasing their dissatisfaction with their housing. Third, a high level of visible exterior housing deterioration on the surrounding block (as measured by the windshield survey) encouraged residents to move away by increasing their housing dissatisfaction.

Although measures of neighborhood quality were important in explaining decisions about moving, demographic characteristics were far more important, accounting for 80 percent of the total variation (Table 6.3). Since earlier studies using metropolitan-wide samples have demonstrated the importance of personal characteristics (Varady, 1983), this finding indicates that many of the moves away from UHD neighborhoods resulted from "normal" causes rather than from factors unique to inner-city areas. The two characteristics of households most strongly associated with moving away were youth and the fact that they were renters rather than homeowners. Younger residents and renters were more likely to move, almost regardless of whether they were satisfied with their housing or were optimistic about the future of the neighborhood. Longer term residents and those with school age children were more likely to stay, although those factors did not have as strong an effect on moving behavior as did youth and renting.

Two other results are interesting because they have been obtained in so few earlier mobility studies. Unskilled workers were more likely to move away, whereas blacks tended to stay. The former finding reflects the instability and low wages of jobs held by unskilled workers, which make it difficult to maintain rental or mortgage payments. In addition, moves by those workers might have resulted from job searches in other cities. Racial differences might also reflect the effect of actual and perceived housing discrimination. Even when blacks were dissatisfied with their houses or pessimistic about their neighborhoods' future, they tended, more than whites, to stay put. They may have thought little was to be gained by searching, since they would not be shown some of the better affordable homes. That finding parallels the one obtained by the author from a national metropolitan sample (Varady, 1983).

One would assume that higher income families would be likely to feel uncomfortable living in lower income neighborhoods, and that that would encourage them to move. While that assumption appears false, low-income families living in high-income neighborhoods were more likely to move. Those moves may have resulted from lower income householders' feeling uncomfortable in those areas; just as likely, however, the lower income families were in neighborhoods where housing costs were increasing rapidly. Cost burdens could have encouraged them to move. With the available data, it is impossible to determine the extent to which the UHD may have caused housing costs to rise.

Given the above explanation, it is surprising that an index measuring the housing cost burden of the family (total housing costs divided by total income) played no meaningful role in the analysis. That result is deceptive. Correlation analyses (not shown) indicate that housing costs did influence people's decision to move, as evidenced by the strong correlation between the likelihood of moving and a high housing cost burden (.26). The latter variable was not a significant predictor in the regression runs because it was intercorrelated with being a low-income family in a high-income neighborhood (.39), which apparently served as a proxy for the existence of a high housing cost burden.

The only measure of housing deterioration which explained moving decisions was the age of the dwelling unit.[4] Those living in older homes were more likely to move because they were more pessimistic about the future of the neighborhood. The results provided no support for the assumption that household density (persons per room) would be correlated with moving.

Goetze's assertion (1976) that confidence in the future of the neighborhood plays a key role in explaining moving decisions in revitalizing neighborhoods is supported. This factor not only formed the path by which the effect of background characteristics was transmitted to moving behavior but also had a statistically significant, independent effect on mobility (beta = .07 in Figure 6.2).

Housing satisfaction, however, played a less important role. While it helped transmit the effect of background characteristics, it did not have a significant independent effect on moving decisions. Additional analyses indicate that housing satisfaction played a far more important role among renters. Renters who were dissatisfied with their homes were far more likely to move than were dissatisfied owners. The latter undoubtedly reflects the high transaction costs experienced by owners seeking to sell (Cox, 1982, p. 118).

Both housing dissatisfaction and neighborhood confidence played less important explanatory roles among whites than blacks (Tables 6.1 and 6.4). Whites who were satisfied with their homes or confident about their neighborhood were almost as likely to move as those who were dissatisfied or pessimistic. These findings imply that many whites made relatively sudden unplanned moves. Some of these moves may have occurred in response to rapid racial change. On the other hand, since many of the whites were elderly, some of the outmigration may have been due to deaths or illnesses. With the limited data available, it is impossible to determine which explanation is more valid.

Conclusion

The Urban Homesteading Demonstration was expected to help raise residents' confidence in their neighborhoods and thereby encourage them to stay. On the contrary, the Demonstration had no significant effect either on confidence or on whether people decided to move away. Living on the same block as a homesteading property did not affect people's decisions on whether to move. It is conceivable that the UHD may have attracted people to move into the area. People moving into such areas might be more sensitive to the presence of the UHD, to the quality of the housing, and, in some cases, to the amenties in the neighborhood than the existing residents were.

These results are bound to disappoint policymakers who contemplate using urban homesteading as a revitalization strategy. Furthermore, they indicate that other housing and neighborhood revitalization programs that involve less visible home improvements are likely to achieve similarly meager results in retaining middle-class families.

Four background characteristics did contribute to residents' decisions to move: youth, holding an unskilled job, having a low-income level in a high-income neighborhood, and perceiving neighbors' property upkeep as inadequate. Six characteristics contributed to residents' decisions to stay: being black, owning their home, being a white family in a predominantly white neighborhood, living in a neighborhood with a high level of social participation, and being optimistic about the neighborhood's future.

This chapter also demonstrates the difficulty in revitalizing racially changing inner-city communities. It would seem necessary to address not only the concerns of whites about racial change but also white and black parents' concerns about the unsuitability of those areas for childrearing. Few tools are available to planners and other public officials to deal with those concerns. Even improving public services does not help keep middle-income families from moving. Where racial change is not an issue, cities could improve residents' confidence in their neighborhood's future, and possibly encourage more residents to stay, by strengthening the social fabric of those neighborhoods and by helping to maintain adequate property upkeep. Cities could promote those goals by organizing residents' associations, by encouraging and supporting neighborhood cleanup campaigns, antilitter patrols, and beautification programs. Those programs may help to increase confidence in the future of the neighborhoods by having a tangible effect on the immediate environment and by contributing to the residents' optimism about the neighborhood's future.

Table 6.1. Determinants of residential mobility (amount of time remained at location after 1977) for total sample, whites, and blacks (Standardized regression coefficients)

Characteristic	Total sample	Whites	Blacks
Owner	.23[a]	.20	.27[a]
Age	.23[a]	.14	.30[a]
Black	.25[a]	—	—
Cost burden	-.06	-.18	.04
Concern about abandonment	.14[a]	.18[a]	.12[a]
Unskilled worker	-.12[a]	-.18[a]	-.12[a]
Neighborhood property values	-.08	.04	-.14[a]
Property upkeep poor	-.12[a]	-.25[a]	-.09[a]
Neighborhood confidence	.08[a]	-.05	.10[a]
Low family income/high neighborhood income	-.13[a]	-.05	-.16[a]
Employed	.07	.03	-.10[a]
High income neighborhood/ good housing conditions	.25[a]	.31	.14
Housing density	.04	.04	.09
Proportion of long-term residents	-.13	-.06	-.13

Characteristic	Total sample	Whites	Blacks
White/neighborhood under 25% black	.16[a]	.22	—
High family income/low neighborhood income	.10	.05	.12
Neighborhood problems	.06	.11	.09[a]
Housing satisfaction	.08[a]	.01	.10[a]
Professional worker	-.08[a]	-.03	-.12[a]
Social interaction	.08[a]	.23[a]	.01
Poor block conditions	-.11[a]	-.12	-.09
Welfare assistance	.05	.13	-.01
Low income neighborhood/ poor housing conditions	.09	.16	-.06
White/neighborhood 50–74% black	.08[a]	.15	[b]
Length of residence	.05	.10	.06
Poor neighborhood housing conditions	.10	.15	.10
Neighborhood poor for childrearing	.05	.16	[b]
Age of house	.03	-.10	.10
Proportion of owners	.03	.12	[b]
Homesteading block	-.02	.04	-.03
Female household head	.03	-.05	.08
Neighborhood repair activity	.03	.12	-.04
Concern about racial change	-.02	-.03	-.03
High income neighborhood/ poor housing conditions	.03	.03	-.02
Neighborhood social cohesiveness	-.01	-.01	-.01

Characteristic	Total sample	Whites	Blacks
Children under 18	.02	.03	.04
Income	b	-.20	.12
White/neighborhood 25–49% black	b	-.04	—
White/neighborhood 75% or more black	b	b	—
Concern about schools	b	.08	-.01
Poor public services	b	-.11	.02
Neighborhood poor for making friends	b	b	-.01
Concern about income change	b	.17^a	-.06
Df	390	133	257
R2	.3387	.3999	.4081

Notes
a. Statistically significant at the .05 level.
b. Not included because it did not meet significance and/or tolerance criteria.

Table 6.2. Indirect, direct and total effects of background characteristics on residential mobility (Amount of time remained at residence after 1977)

Characteristic	Indirect effects	Direct effects	Total effects
Black	.00	.17	.17
Age	.00	.24	.24
Unskilled worker	.01	-.11	-.10
High family income/high neighborhood income	-.01	.00	-.01
Low family income/high neighborhood income	.00	-.11	-.11
Owner	.01	.26	.27

Characteristic	Indirect effects	Direct effects	Total effects
Children under 18	-.01	.00	-.01
White/neighborhood under 25% black	.00	.08	.08
White/neighborhood 50–74% black	.00	.00	.00
Length of residence	.01	.00	.01
Age of house	-.01	.00	-.01
Proportion of long term residents	.00	-.07	-.07
Proportion of owners	.02	.00	.02
Neighborhood property values	-.01	.01	.00
Neighborhood repair activity	-.01	.00	-.01
Low income neighborhood/ poor housing conditions	-.01	.00	-.01
Poor neighborhood housing conditions	-.01	.00	-.01
Social interaction	.01	.07	.08
Neighborhood social cohesiveness	.01	.00	.01
Neighborhood problems	-.01	.00	-.01
Concern about racial change	.00	.00	.00
Property upkeep inadequate	-.01	-.08	-.09
Concern about abandoned properties	.00	.14	.14
Neighborhood poor for childrearing	-.01	.00	-.01

Note
The above results have been rounded to the nearest hundredth.
Those reported as ".00" represent very small but real indirect effects.

Table 6.3. Total R2 and Partial R2 for background characteristics on residential mobility (Amount of time remained after 1977)

Variable set	Total R2	Partial R2
Demographic characteristics	.2696	.2696
Objective housing characteristics (over and beyond demographic characteristics	.2726	.0041
Neighborhood assessments (over and beyond demographic and housing characteristics)	.3268	.0773
Neighborhood confidence and housing satisfaction (over and beyond demographic, housing characteristics and neighborhood assessments)	.3387	.0147

Table 6.4. Impact of housing dissatisfaction and neighborhood confidence on residential mobility, controlling for race (Proportion moving)

	Whites	Sig.	Blacks	Sig.
Housing satis.				
Not satisfied	33% (46)	n.s.	29% (18)	.000
Satisfied	22%(224)		12%(329)	
Neighborhood Confidence				
Not Optimistic	26%(170)	n.s.	22%(224)	.03
Optimistic	21% (97)		14%(254)	

Chapter 7

Housing Repairs

When the Urban Homesteading Demonstration was introduced in the mid-1970s, it was expected to induce nonparticipating neighbors to improve their own properties. This chapter tests whether homesteading achieved this goal, by determining whether respondents living on homesteading blocks spent more on repairs and improvements than those living farther away, when other relevant background characteristics are controlled. It is assumed that families living near homesteading properties would be more likely to be aware of the program, making them more optimistic about the future of the neighborhood and more likely to make repairs and improvements. Although the main aim of the chapter is to evaluate the Urban Homesteading Demonstration, it also seeks to contribute to the limited available knowledge on the determinants of housing repairs in declining inner-city areas.

First, economists have viewed housing repair decisions as a type of optimizing behavior. That is, individuals seek to maintain or improve their homes in order to maximize their short-term and long-term well-being. Second, it is assumed that the repair decision involves both consumption and investment components. More specifically, the improvements not only increase the level of services provided by the dwelling (e.g., more space, better heating, and so on), they may also increase the resale value of the property. Third, it is posited that *expectations* regarding interest rates, housing deterioration and neighborhood population changes play a key role in repair decisions. Finally, repair and mobility decisions are assumed to be closely interrelated. A family anticipating moving in the near future may make only the cosmetic repairs necessary to sell the home and avoid needed major repairs. The analysis that follows incorporates all of these assumptions from earlier writings.

Despite the considerable interest in the subject by social scientists, there have been relatively few empirical studies of repair decision making among single family homeowners (Mendelsohn, 1977; D. Myers, 1984; Shear and Carpenter, 1982). These studies, while helpful, have three weaknesses. First, they rely on metropolitan-wide samples and provide limited insight into repair decision making among inner-city residents. Second, the role of the neighborhood context is either ignored or deemphasized. Finally, these studies fail to examine the role of householder evaluations such as housing satisfaction and neighborhood confidence in these decisions.

This chapter addresses these weaknesses through secondary analysis of the Urban Homesteading Demonstration neighborhood residents data set. As mentioned earlier, the UHD data set draws from a wide national cross section of inner-city neighborhoods and includes a wide variety of subjective, as well as objective, measures of neighborhood conditions. Further, in contrast to earlier studies which focus exclusively on the direct effects of background characteristics, this chapter tests for the indirect effects of background factors, as well (i.e., the flow of influence of these variables through housing and neighborhood evaluations).

The housing repair model used in this chapter, similar to the mobility model in Chapter 6, includes three types of variables: (1) background personal, housing, and neighborhood characteristics; (2) housing satisfaction and neighborhood confidence; and (3) the amount spent on repairs. See Table 7.1 for a listing of the variables included in the analysis and Appendix Table 1 for definitions of these variables. It is assumed that the background characteristics may affect repairs indirectly or directly. For example, as a result of living in dilapidated housing, lower income families may be more dissatisfied and consequently more likely to make repairs. On the other hand, insufficient resources may prevent families from making needed repairs, regardless of the level of dissatisfaction or perceived need (a direct effect). One of the aims of this chapter is to compare the relative importance of the indirect and direct effects of different background characteristics.

The chapter adds to the limited behavioral research on the impacts of government housing rehabilitation programs on the repair decisions of neighboring families. Pedone (1982) found that awareness of the Neighborhood Housing Service (NHS) program did not increase either the probability of making a major repair or the level of expenditure on major repairs among householders who were not clients of the NHS program. In contrast, R. Ginsberg (1983, p. 6–18) found that concentrated housing rehabilitation activity, as part of the Community Development Block Grant program, did promote improvements but only among those living in the immediate area.

> One thousand dollars' worth of assistance given as grants within a respondent's grid square (i.e., within 1/16 mile) generates about $100 in repairs or maintenance.

The chapter builds upon earlier analyses of the determinants of repairs in the UHD by Pedone, Remch and Case, 1980 by: (1) testing for the indirect, as well as direct, effects of background characteristics; (2) utilizing 1980, as well as 1970, census data in measuring neighborhood change, and (3) more stringently testing for the impact of homesteading activity. That is, this chapter's analysis is limited to householders remaining over the two-year period of the Demonstration. The analytic strategy is to use objective and subjective characteristics measured in 1977 to predict expenditures over the 1977 to 1979 period. Since those living on homesteading blocks would have been exposed to program activity for at least two years, the proximity variable would be a reasonable indicator for awareness of the program. If Urban Homesteading is not shown to have an effect on the repair decisions of householders in this "stable" sample present for two years, it is improbable that it would have an impact on the larger and more transient UHD sample as a whole.

This approach has two significant disadvantages, however. First, by limiting the analysis to homeowners remaining over the two years, we exclude the role inmigrating families can play in neighborhood improvement. Second, the exclusion of inmigrants results in a serious loss of data. That is, the analysis discussed below is based on 199 cases. Appendix Tables 2 and 3 show, however, that this exclusion does not introduce any serious bias, since the characteristics of householders in the regression sample resemble fairly closely the characteristics of those in the UHD sample as a whole.[1]

Methods

The analytic approach in this chapter is similar to that in the last two chapters. Regression analyses to explain repair expenditures were run in two steps. First, the background characteristics were used to predict housing satisfaction; next, the background characteristics *plus* housing satisfaction were used to predict repair expenditures. Neighborhood confidence was not included because it did not play a meaningful explanatory role, a point elaborated upon below. Table 7.1 presents these results for all of the variables hypothesized to affect the repair decision. The regressions were rerun, including only those variables that were statistically significant. The results are presented in a path diagram (Figure 7.1) and summarized in Table 7.2.

Housing repair expenditures were measured by an index formed by summing the total household expenditures between waves 1 and 2 and between waves 2 and 3. The average over the two-year period was $1,702. Approximately two-fifths (38 percent) spent little (i.e., below $300) on repairs both years, and about the same proportion (41 percent) made major repairs (i.e., spent $300 or more) during one of the years only. The remainder made major repairs during both years.[2]

As mentioned above, the regression analysis is based on the 199 cases of owners remaining during the two-year period, for whom full information was available on all independent variables in the repair model.

Findings

In contrast to expectations, Urban Homesteading did not promote housing repairs and improvements among nonparticipating

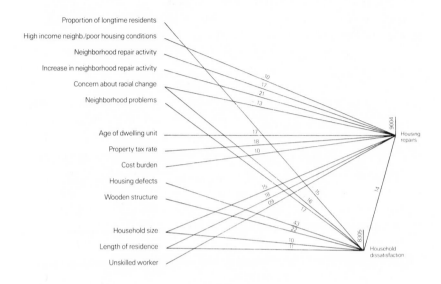

Figure 7.1   **Path diagram, determinants of repair activity (amount spent on repairs 1977-1979).**

Note: All betas are statistically significant at the .05 level.

families. Living on the same block as a homesteading property did not make residents more likely to make home improvements. The proximity variable did not meet tolerance and significance criteria and was not included in the initial regression equation.

It would be incorrect, however, to infer from the preceding that the neighborhood environment had no effect on home repair decisions. In fact, of the four groups of variables tested (Table 7.3), objective and subjective measures of neighborhood conditions was the most important, explaining about one-half of the variation in expenditures. The results provide additional evidence to that in earlier chapters on the adverse impact of demographic change on revitalization efforts. The concern about racial change directly reduced home repair expenditures. Table 7.1 shows that this concern was particularly influential among blacks. Perhaps some middle-income blacks who had recently arrived in these neighborhoods were concerned about the spread of ghetto problems into their neighborhood (e.g., increased crime, falling test scores), and this concern may have made them less likely to invest. This speculation is based on Leven et al.'s 1976 study of neighborhood change in St. Louis. Furthermore, earlier chapters of this book showed that there was some realistic basis for householders' being concerned about racial change being followed by income and class change.

Although the concern about racial change played an important explanatory role, the objective indicators of racial change did not (e.g., the increase in the proportion of blacks in the neighborhood between 1970 and 1980). The insignificant results probably reflect neighbors often evaluating the same population shift differently. Clearly, it is the *evaluation*, rather than the objective reality which is critical in influencing the repair decision.[3]

Figure 7.1 shows, somewhat surprisingly, that those who were most concerned about racial change tended to be most satisfied with their homes. It is possible that some of the householders, particularly the elderly, who found population shifts distressing, adjusted by spending more time at home. Being satisfied with the home was one way in which they coped with an adverse residential environment.[4]

Other regression results, while not quite statistically significant and therefore not reflected in the path diagram, are strong enough, taken together, to suggest that the social fabric influences repair decisions. Those who perceived the neighborhood as poor for childrearing or who perceived the property upkeep of neighbors as inadequate (indicating a decline in neighborhood social cohesion) spent less on repairs than those who did not perceive these problems.

Although the Urban Homesteading Demonstration did not have the expected spillover effects, resident repair decisions were influenced by the presence of concentrated rehabilitation activity in the surrounding area (unrelated to the Demonstration).[5] Respondents living in neighborhoods with high levels of repair activity, or in ones that experienced large proportional increases in rehabilitation activity between 1977 and 1979, spent more on repairs and improvements than those living in other neighborhoods, controlling for other background characteristics. Exposure to and awareness of this rehabilitation may have convinced householders that their own investments in housing improvements would be repaid in the form of higher resale value. Comparing this significant result with the insignificant finding for the proximity to homesteading variable highlights the importance of *concentrated* rehabilitation activity. It appears that rehabilitation has to be of a sufficient density (i.e., more than one or two houses on a block) to have an impact on neighbors. This result parallels findings from the recent CDBG study discussed above (R. Ginsberg, 1983).

Although perceived ethnic shifts did impede housing repairs, the existence of neighborhood physical problems did not. In contrast to what had been anticipated, the objective and subjective measures of neighborhood physical problems (e.g., a high proportion of old buildings, a concern about abandoned dwellings) generally did not have strong negative impacts on expenditures. In fact, the perception of neighborhood physical problems had a relatively strong (although not statistically significant) positive impact on expenditures. Apparently, respondents did not see problems such as potholes and litter as obstacles to improvement, as long as the population was stable (with a relatively high income level or experiencing significant middle-income inmigration). The latter point is reinforced by the finding that residents of neighborhoods with relatively high income levels and poor property conditions were particularly likely to invest in repairs and improvements. Residents of these neighborhoods probably saw vacant or poorly maintained properties as "opportunities" for middle-income investors and not as obstacles to community betterment.

In contrast to what had been expected, two measures of overall community viability and attractiveness (neighborhood property values and changes in these values) played no meaningful explanatory role.[6]

Previous research (Ahlbrandt and Cunningham, 1979; Galster and Hesser, 1982) emphasizes the importance of the neighborhood's social fabric in influencing repair decisions. That is, in tightly knit communities residents would experience strong peer pressure to maintain their homes to the same level as their neighbor's homes. This hypothesis was not supported by the UHD data. Neither the perception of a cohesive neighborhood nor the proportion of owners (an indicator of a cohesive neighborhood) played a significant role in the analysis. Further, the proportion of long-term residents (an indicator of a cohesive neighborhood) had a small negative impact on repair expenditures, rather than the positive one which was anticipated. Perhaps the insignificant results for the social cohesion variables reflect the racial change occurring in many of the UHD communities. As a result of the rapid population flux, residents may not have known neighbors long and well enough to pressure them to make needed repairs. It is impossible to predict whether such strong social patterns would develop over time. Finally, there was no backing for our hypothesis that those who were most active in their neighborhood would spend the most, regardless of the degree of neighborhood social cohesiveness.

The results provide additional evidence of the limited role that government programs can play in neighborhood revitalization. Neither the quality of public services in general nor the quality of the public schools had a significant impact on repair decisions.

Not surprisingly, housing characteristics played a key role in influencing repair decisions, with the age of the home being the most important predictor. Older homes deteriorate more quickly, increasing the necessity of making repairs. Furthermore, many of the owners of older dwellings undoubtedly felt the need to modernize. In addition, those in homes with one or more defects (e.g., the heating system, plumbing, electrical system, roof, exterior) or in ones made of wood were more likely to be dissatisfied and hence spent more. The latter finding reflects the more rapid deterioration of wooden than either brick or stucco exteriors.

We had anticipated that high property tax rates would discourage owners from making major improvements because they might expect taxes to rise sharply following a reappraisal. In fact, this factor had a strong direct positive impact on repairs, rather than the negative impact which was anticipated, implying that few owners expected such reappraisals, a point stressed in two recent studies (Mayer, 1984; Shear and Carpenter, 1982). The significant positive beta coefficient is difficult to explain. Perhaps, the property tax variable served as a proxy for housing and neighborhood conditions not measured on the survey.

Three other housing characteristics did not have the hypothesized effects or repair expenditures. Those in larger homes (i.e., with many rooms) did not have a greater need for repairs, and those who had made major repairs the year prior to the Demonstration did not spend less over the succeeding two years. Finally, there was no evidence that owner occupants in multiunit structures were better able to afford repair costs as a result of rental income.

Personal characteristics also played an influential role, affecting both the perceived need for repairs and the ability to carry out the repairs. As expected, recent arrivals spent more than long-term residents reflecting the tendency for the former to modernize or otherwise improve their homes to make them more suitable to their tastes. Also as anticipated, those with a high housing cost burden (mortgage plus utilities divided by income) had less disposable income available and spent less on repairs. However, there was little support for the hypothesis that those with few housing options would have lower aspiration levels, would be less critical of the home, and would spend less on property repairs. Blacks, welfare recipients, and female-headed households did not, as predicted, spend less on repairs and improvements than other householders. In direct contradiction to expectations, unskilled workers spent significantly more on repairs than professionals, when other background characteristics were controlled. Perhaps as a result of the limited opportunities for moving to a better home, unskilled workers adjusted to housing defects by remaining and making repairs.[7]

We had expected larger families to spend less, reflecting the greater availability of family members to work on repairs; but this factor had a strong positive effect on expenditures (Figure 7.1). The result probably reflects the "greater wear and tear" on dwellings occupied by large families. In addition, the greater repair expenditures may reflect the limited opportunities for moving, due to the paucity of large inexpensive single family homes.[8]

It seemed likely that the elderly would spend less for repairs, holding other factors constant, because they would be unwilling to incur the debts associated with major repair jobs. In fact, age played an insignificant role in the regression analysis.[9] Age-related factors leading to reduced expenditures may have been counterbalanced by the greater reliance of the elderly on contractors for needed repairs.

Housing dissatisfaction played the expected role in the housing repairs model, in transmitting the impact of background characteristics through to repair behavior. Furthermore, housing dissatisfaction had a direct impact, even when other relevant characteristics were controlled (beta = .14), reflecting the influence of personal, housing, and neighborhood characteristics not included in the model.

However, the neighborhood confidence variable did not play the expected role in transmitting background information. A separate regression, limited to this variable alone, explained almost none of the variation in expenditures; further, there was only a weak negative correlation (−.02) between optimism and repairs, rather than the strong positive correlation that was anticipated. The tendency for some of those who were pessimistic, and, hence, who anticipated moving, to make modest repairs to increase the saleability of their property apparently counteracted the propensity of some of those who were confident in their neighborhood's future to make property improvements. Unfortunately, with the limited data from the survey, it is impossible to verify this interpretation.

Conclusion

This chapter provides additional evidence to that in the earlier ones on the lack of spillover effects of the Urban Homesteading Demonstration. Contrary to the hopes of program advocates, homesteading did not induce nonparticipating neighbors to improve their own properties. The absence of spillovers probably resulted, in part, from the insufficient density of homesteading activity.

In making repair decisions, homeowners were, however, sensitive to what was taking place in the surrounding neighborhood. High levels of repair activity and increases in such activity which were unrelated to the Urban Homesteading Demonstration assured owners that repairs would lead to increases in the resale value of their homes. Conversely, concerns about racial change and the spread of ghetto problems into their community made owners reluctant to make property investments. In contrast, the existence of neighborhood physical problems had little impact on repair decisions.

The results provide mixed support for the hypothesized importance of a number of background personal and housing characteristics. As expected, recent arrivals and those in older homes, wooden ones or ones with defects, tended to spend more, while those with a high cost burden spent less. In contrast to expectations, the unskilled and those with high tax rates spent more on home repairs than others.

Finally, the analysis provided mixed support for the repair model developed earlier in the chapter. While housing satisfaction did play the expected role between background characteristics and repairs, neighborhood confidence played no meaningful role in the analysis.

Table 7.1. Determinants of home repair activity among owners (total amount spent on home 1977 to 1979) for total sample, whites and blacks (Standardized regression coefficients)

Characteristic	Total sample	Whites	Blacks
Family size	.14[a]	.11	.09
Housing satisfaction	-.12[a]	-.05	-.16
Age of building	.16[a]	.41[a]	.04
Length of residence	-.16[a]	-.08	-.22
Neighborhood poor for childrearing	-.11	-.18	-.22[a]
Property tax rate	.16[a]	-.04	.25
Increase in neighborhood repair activity	.30[a]	.06	.25[a]
Neighborhood repair activity	.27[a]	c	c
High income neighborhood/ poor housing conditions	.26[a]	-.15	-.03
Concern about racial change	-.13[a]	.09	-.22[a]

Characteristic	Total sample	Whites	Blacks
Neighborhood problems	.14[a]	.05	.13
Neighborhood poor for friendships	-.11	[b]	-.04
Unskilled worker	.11[a]	.43[a]	.02
Property upkeep	-.10[a]	-.08	.02
Welfare assistance	.10	-.15	.17[a]
Cost burden	-.14[a]	-.03	-.45[a]
Concern about schools	-.09	-.04	-.12
Proportion of long term residents	-.08	-.46	.19
Poor property conditions	-.02	[c]	[c]
Female household head	.07	-.12	.08
White/neighborhood 25–49% black	-.07	-.27	—
Highest grade	.06	.14	.06
Professional worker	-.06	-.11	-.04
Proportion of owners	.06	-.35	.06
Concern about abandonment	.04	-.04	.06
Housing defects	.06	-.02	.11
Poor neighborhood services	-.06	.09	-.04
Number of rooms	-.02	-.14	.15
White/neighborhood under 25% black	.11	-.43	—
Neighborhood proportion black	.14	-.32	.15
Proportion of old buildings	.16	-.02	.05
Change in property values	-.13	-.13	-.02
Employed	.05	[b]	.03
Neighborhood property values	.07	.07	.25

Characteristic	Total sample	Whites	Blacks
Concern about income change	.02	-.04	[b]
Wooden construction	.02	-.07	.07
Poor block conditions	-.05	.50	-.08
High income neighborhood/ good housing conditions	.14	.19	-.32[a]
Low income neighborhood/ poor housing conditions	.15	-.02	-.24
Increase in neighborhood proportion black	-.06	-.29	.23
Social interaction	.01	-.23	.15
Neighborhood confidence	.01	.24	-.07
Multiunit structure	-.02	[b]	-.07
White/neighborhood 50–74% black	-.01	-.09	—
Young children	.01	.22	-.07
Age	[b]	.07	-.10
Homesteading block	[b]	-.32[a]	.07
Black	[b]	—	—
Income	[b]	-.04	-.29[a]
Repairs previous year	[b]	.16	-.02
Neighborhood social cohesiveness	[b]	.08	-.06
Df	199	78	121
R2	.29	.44	.44

Notes:
a. Statistically significant at the .05 level.
b. Variable failed to meet tolerance or significance criteria and was not included in regression equation.
c. Variable was highly intercorrelated with one or more other variables in the white/black sample and, therefore, was excluded from the regression analysis.

Table 7.2. Indirect, direct, and total effects of background characteristics on repair activity for owners

Characteristic	Indirect	Direct	Total
Proportion of long time residents	-.02	—	-.02
High income neighborhood/ poor housing conditions	—	.10	.10
Neighborhood repair activity	—	.17	.17
Increase in neighborhood repair activity	—	.21	.21
Concern about racial change	—	-.13	-.13
Neighborhood problems	.02	—	.02
Age of dwelling unit	—	.17	.17
Property tax rate	—	.18	.18
Cost burden	—	-.11	-.11
Housing defects	.06	.06	
Wooden structure	.03	—	.03
Household size	-.01	.15	.14
Length of residence	-.03	-.18	-.21
Unskilled worker	—	.09	.09

Table 7.3. Total R2 and Partial R2 for background characteristics on repair activity (total amount spent on repairs between 1977 and 1979)

Variable set	Total R2	Partial R2
Demographic characteristics	.0822	.0822
Housing characteristics (over and beyond demographic characteristics)	.1511	.0729
Neighborhood characteristics (over and beyond demographic and housing characteristics)	.2688	.1387
Housing satisfaction and neighborhood confidence (over and beyond demographic, housing and neighborhood characteristics	.2774	.0117

Chapter 8

How Do The Elderly Fare in Homesteading Neighborhoods?

The image of the elderly in urban neighborhoods has been largely negative. They are perceived as socially isolated individuals living in deteriorating housing and plagued by violent street crime. Neighborhood conservation programs like Urban Homesteading offer the prospect of a new image for the inner-city elderly, the effects of revitalization programs benefiting them through better shopping and less crime. On the other hand, there is a fear that such revitalization programs will hurt the more susceptible elderly (e.g., the "old-old," those with extremely low incomes) by promoting higher housing costs and by disrupting long-established social patterns. Clearly, there is a need for research to determine the extent to which the elderly have been helped or hurt by such conservation programs. (P. Myers, 1978 and 1982).

Pedone, Remch, and Case's 1980 evaluation of the UHD concluded that these neighborhoods were experiencing increases in housing values and in rehabilitation activity.[1] However, USR&E did not investigate the impact of the Demonstration on subgroups such as the elderly within the target population. This is the aim of the present chapter.

Specifically, this chapter seeks to answer three questions. First, to what extent did the housing and neighborhood conditions of the elderly at the start of the UHD support the widely accepted stereotypes of the elderly living in inner-city neighborhoods? Second, to what extent were elderly individuals and couples more likely than younger families to benefit from improved neighborhood conditions such as repaired streets, better police protection, and improved public transportation, and to what extent were they more likely to be hurt by rising housing costs and changed social patterns? Finally, to what extent were particular subgroups within the elderly population (for instance, those with very low incomes) most likely to be helped or hurt by revitalization?

Methods

This research consists of secondary analysis of the longitudinal Urban Homesteading Demonstration Neighborhood Residents Survey data set. A series of indices were created to measure changes in perceptions of neighborhood conditions between 1977 and 1979. The indices were created by crosstabulating variables measuring particular neighborhood evaluations for 1979 by the corresponding 1977 factors. The resulting indices had four categories: (1) no problem existed at either point in time; (2) perceived problem in 1979, but not in 1977; (3) perceived problem in 1977, but not in 1979; (4) no change, problem existed at both points in time. The results (not presented here) indicate that there was considerable attitudinal shifting between 1977 and 1979. Depending on the particular attitude, between one-fifth and one-third of the respondents became either more positive or more negative, while the remainder held the same view at both points in time. Crosstabular analysis is used to examine the relation between these indices (recoded to only include cases where change occurred) and the age of the household head (whether "under 65" or "65 and older"). It also examines the relation between these indices and a set of objective personal characteristics for elderly respondents only. The crosstabular runs were restricted to those cases in which the same respondent or a member of the same household completed the interviews in wave 1 and wave 3.

Findings

A. How serious were housing and neighborhood problems at the beginning of the Demonstration?

Based on previous studies of the elderly in revitalizing neighborhoods, we suspected that the elderly would be poorer, more likely to live alone, and would have lived longer at their locations than younger families (P. Myers, 1978 and 1982). These assumptions were supported. The mean household income for the elderly (total for all household members before taxes), $6,610, was about one-half that for the nonelderly, $12,399 (p < .0000). A far smaller proportion of elderly were married with the spouse present (50 percent of 98 respondents versus 69 percent of 551 respondents, p < .005). Finally, the average length of residence for the elderly, 24 years, was almost three times as great as for the nonelderly, 9 years (p < .0000). We supposed that a larger proportion of elderly would be renters (and living in apartments), but this was not the case. About four-fifths of both age groups owned their own homes. The only other major difference between the elderly and the nonelderly was race; the elderly were more likely to be white (71 percent, 98, versus 29 percent, 546, p < .0000). This latter difference reflects racial changes that occurred in many of the UHD neighborhoods during the 1960s and 1970s and the often-noted tendency for the elderly to remain when out-migration occurs.

In contradiction to the stereotypical image of the socially isolated elderly, we anticipated that the extended tenure of the elderly would lead to especially high levels of social interaction in the surrounding neighborhood. Neither our expectations nor the stereotype was supported. There were only slight differences between members of the two age groups when an index, which combined how often the respondent got together with neighbors on the block and how many of the neighbors he felt he knew well enough to stop and talk with, was analyzed.

We expected elderly men to be less active socially in their surrounding neighborhood than elderly women. The men would be used to developing friendships on the job and, having retired, would have some difficulty finding friends in the immediate area.

In contrast, we expected the women to maintain the same type of social life that they had enjoyed in earlier years, one based on friends from the surrounding community. In fact, there were insignificant differences between elderly men and women in neighborhood social patterns (i.e., the number of neighbors that they knew well enough to speak to and the frequency of contact). Apparently, many of the elderly men had taken advantage of the free time made available by retirement to meet and talk to neighbors. In sharp contrast, among younger householders, women were more active socially than men. Due to space limitations on the survey, it was not possible to investigate informal social patterns beyond these two questions.

As a result of the fact that many of the elderly live on fixed incomes from social security or pensions, it was believed that even with government-mandated cost of living increases, they would find it particularly difficult to cope with inflationary housing costs. Consequently, it was assumed that the elderly would have a higher housing cost burden than the nonelderly. An index to measure cost burden was computed by dividing total housing costs by total family income. Contrary to expectations, the cost burden was about the same for the two groups (28 percent). Viewed another way, about 45 percent of both groups spent one-quarter or more of their incomes for housing costs. Even when the analysis was limited to renters, there were insignificant differences between older and younger families. This latter result may reflect the frequently observed tendency for landlords to provide elderly families with substantial rent discounts because they have lived in the same unit for such a long time and/or because they cause less trouble and damage than younger families (see, for example, Ferguson, Holin, and Moss, undated, p. 330–331).

The stereotype, that the elderly are "empty nesters" and "overhoused" (P. Myers, 1982), was supported. Household density was nearly twice as high for younger as for older families (.67 versus .36, $p < .0000$). This difference reflects the tendency for the elderly to remain, even after their children have left home. Because it is easier for renters to move when they have too much space, we had expected this tendency to move to a small space to be more pronounced between younger than older renters than between younger and older owners. This assertion was not supported however. The image of the elderly living in deteriorating housing was not supported.[2] A higher proportion of younger (one-fifth) than older (one-tenth) families rated one or more of the following features of their dwellings as inadequate: walls, ceilings and floors, heating system, plumbing system, electrical system, the roof, and the exterior paint or siding. Furthermore, a higher proportion of elderly than nonelderly families rated the overall condition of the home as good, on a scale of good, satisfactory, poor (87 percent, 98, versus 79 percent, 549, $p < .09$). These surprising results may reflect the fact that the elderly have lived so long at their current locations that they have developed strong social attachments there, producing higher levels of satisfaction. It is also likely that older families expected less from their homes and were satisfied living in conditions which younger families would have considered unsatisfactory. Finally, low housing costs and accessibility to transportation, services, and facilities probably constituted additional reasons for remaining in objectively substandard neighborhoods and homes (Bild and Havighurst, 1976; Neibanck and Yessian, 1968; and Struyk, 1976, as cited in P. Myers, 1978).

Although the expected differences in the perception of housing problems did not exist, age produced sharp differences in the propensity to make property improvements. The mean number of property investments made annually by younger families was 50 percent higher than for older ones (1.9 versus 1.3, $p < .002$). further, among those who did make at least one housing investment, the average amount spent annually was nearly twice as great for younger as for older families ($1,185 versus $680, not significant). The differences in property investments are not attributable to the lower income levels of elderly households. When older and younger households in the same income category were compared, the former made fewer property improvements and spent less on them. There are two other possible explanations for these differences. First, the elderly may have become accommodated to inadequate conditions, or they may have had lower standards to start with, leading to less of a perceived need for repairs. Second, even in those cases where elderly householders saw the need, they may have been reluctant to incur the obligations of long-term home improvement loans.[3]

The notion that the elderly would be more susceptible to

street crime and, consequently, would be more likely to perceive it as a problem was not supported. Virtually identical proportions (about one-third) of the elderly and nonelderly householders viewed crime as a serious problem. Furthermore, the elderly were less likely to be burglarized (14 percent, 98, versus 24 percent, 85, p < .05). Paralleling the results for crime and supporting the findings of the 1980–1982 Urban Institute and Conservation Foundation survey (P. Myers, 1982), the elderly were more likely to view overall neighborhood conditions as satisfactory. For example, a somewhat higher proportion of older respondents perceived their neighborhood as having none of the following problems: street noise, dangerous street traffic, streets or roads in need of repair, inadequate or poor street lighting, trash, litter or junk in the street, people living in houses that were run down, or crime. In addition, there were insignificant differences by age in optimism about the neighborhood's future (an index based on two questions: the overall quality of the neighborhood, and the expected direction of change over the next three years). About one-half of old and young householders were optimistic (e.g., neighborhood "so-so" but expected it to get better), one-fourth were neither optimistic nor pessimistic, and one-fourth were pessimistic. These results imply that the residential environments in these neighborhoods were not as threatening as is often supposed. However, another explanation is possible. The elderly may have accommodated themselves to living in their poor environments because they perceived that they had few choices available.

During the early and mid-1970s, many cities were forced to cut back public services. Some of the cuts were thought to be particularly deleterious on the elderly, such as police protection and public transit. We expected that the elderly would be particularly concerned about poor public services, but the results did not support this expectation. Older respondents tended to be more satisfied with public services than younger ones. Nearly one-half of the elderly (48 percent, 92) were satisfied with all five services listed on the questionnaire: police, neighborhood shopping, garbage collection, parks and recreation, public transportation. This was true for only a little over one-third of the younger families (36 percent, 526, p < .04). The only service with which the elderly were more likely to be dissatisfied was neighborhood shopping, and here the differences were not statistically significant. In contrast to expectations, a significantly higher proportion of the elderly were satisfied with police protection (87 percent, 97, versus 73 percent, 546, p < .007). Finally, given the history of racial change in many of the UHD neighborhoods and that a disproportionately large number of the elderly were white, it was expected that many of the elderly would be concerned about racial shifts in their immediate areas. This was, in fact, the case. Whereas 30 percent (96) of the older respondents were concerned about these changes, only 19 percent (544) of the younger ones were concerned (p < .04).

B. Were the elderly disproportionately affected by revitalization?

During the 1977–1979 period, some of the UHD neighborhoods were experiencing signs of revitalization with respect to housing prices and housing rehabilitation activity. There was, however, far less evidence of revitalization in terms of block housing and environmental conditions, as measured by the windshield surveys. Environmental conditions (e.g., road surfaces, curbs, sidewalks) deteriorated somewhat, while exterior conditions of housing improved slightly.

This limited revitalization did not disproportionately hurt or help the elderly. Revitalization did not have an especially harmful impact on the elderly due to the combination of rising housing costs and fixed income levels. An index dividing 1979 by 1977 cost burdens indicated the same change for older and younger households (i.e., 1.11). Even when the analysis was limited to renters, there were insignificant differences by age group.

Additional insight into the issue of whether the elderly were disproportionately affected by revitalization activities is provided by the results of a series of questions asking renters about the direction and the amount of change in rental costs during the preceding year and about likely changes during the next year. Owners were asked about the direction and the amount of change in property taxes.

In contrast to the rest of the chapter (which is based on the longitudinal UHD data set), this section is based on separate analyses of the wave 1 and wave 3 data sets. This was done because the results for the questions on past and future cost increases were included in the wave 1 and 3 data sets but not the longitudinal set. The findings should be considered tentative, since the comparisons using these two sets do not necessarily involve the same families due to in- and outmigration.

There was no evidence to support fears of the elderly being hurt disproportionately by escalating rents. Whereas in 1977 the elderly were more likely to have experienced recent increases in rents, by 1979 there were virtually no differences between the elderly and the nonelderly in perceptions of recent increases. Furthermore, over the course of the Demonstration, the elderly did not become more likely to anticipate future increases. For both young and old householders, the proportion anticipating increases rose slowly, so that by 1979 a little more than one-third expected such increases over the next year.

There was also no support for the concern that the elderly would be hurt disproportionately by rising property taxes. Between 1976 and 1977, the elderly experienced only a slightly smaller increase in taxes ($90) than younger householders ($100). In contrast, between 1978 and 1979, younger householders experienced a far larger increase ($162 versus $34). A similar trend is apparent with respect to differences in expectations of future increases in property taxes (an $18 gap in 1977, widening to an $111 gap in 1979).

On the average, the elderly owned homes of lower value, hence their taxes were lower. This implies that the small increases in property taxes over the course of the Demonstration might have had a great impact. In order to measure the impact of these increases more precisely, an index was computed by dividing the anticipated property tax increase by the then current property tax level. Contrary to the stereotype, the ratios rose more rapidly for younger than older families (.13 to .22 versus .11 to .14) implying that property taxes were becoming more of a burden for younger people.

It was assumed that if revitalization led to the replacement of many long-term residents by newer families, the familiar social patterns of the elderly could be disrupted. However, this concern was not supported. Younger and older householders were similarly likely to experience decreased social interaction during this period, and similar proportions perceived that their neighborhood had become a worse place for making friends. As Cantor's study (cited in P. Myers, 1982) indicates, since the elderly are more dependent on the local neighborhood to meet their daily needs, they could be considered to be more sensitive to any changes that might occur. Consequently, over the two-year period between wave 1 and wave 3 of the UHD evaluation study, it was believed the elderly would be more likely to perceive improvements in their neighborhoods. Although the results are mixed, they tend not to support this assumption. Among householders who perceived changes in neighborhood conditions, it was the younger ones who were more likely to perceive a reduction in the number of neighborhood environmental problems (43 percent, 166, versus 32 percent, 28, n.s.). Younger families were also more likely to perceive a decrease in the incidence of street crime. In contrast, and in support of the hypothesis, older families were somewhat more likely to perceive an improvement in public services (57 percent, 30, versus 48 percent, 173, n.s.).

Similarly, since (as noted earlier) the elderly tended to be more concerned about racial shifts, they would presumably be more likely to perceive changes in racial composition. In fact, there were virtually no differences between the elderly and the nonelderly in the likelihood of becoming less concerned about racial shifts over this two-year period.

These results, which indicate that revitalization did not have disproportionately greater impacts on the elderly, could be misleading. It is possible that a larger proportion of older families lived in UHD neighborhoods experiencing few if any signs of revitalization. If so, this would have led to small increases in housing cost burdens and little change in neighborhood quality. It was hypothesized that, if we limited our analysis to residents of neighborhoods experiencing rapid revitalization, sharper differences between young and old families would be shown.

This hypothesis was not supported in analyses limited to residents of UHD neighborhoods experiencing the most rapid increases in housing rehabilitation activity. In contrast to what was anticipated, it was the younger families which experienced the largest increases in housing cost burdens: a mean of 1.13 (163)

versus 1.01 (26), n.s. Furthermore, the elderly were not more likely to be hurt by declines in levels of social participation. The only
evidence supporting this hypothesis related to changes in the
rating of the neighborhood for making friends. Nearly two-thirds
(63 percent, 16) of the elderly who changed their rating, felt their
neighborhood had become worse, as compared to only two-fifths
(41 percent, 109, n.s.) of younger families.

There was inconclusive support for the assertion that elderly
residents of such neighborhoods would be more likely to perceive
improvements in neighborhood conditions. In fact, younger
families generally were more likely to hold such beliefs. Specifically, among householders who perceived changes in the seriousness
of neighborhood environmental problems, younger ones were
more likely to perceive a decrease in the number of such problems: 51 percent (85) versus 33 percent (15), n.s. Furthermore,
younger families were significantly more likely to perceive a
decline in the seriousness of crime, 65 percent (103) versus 32
percent (19), p < .01. The only finding in support of the above
assertions had to do with public services. The elderly were
somewhat more likely to perceive such improvements. Among the
elderly who perceived changes in the quality of public services,
almost three-fourths (71 percent, 77) perceived improvements.
This was true for less than one-half (44 percent, 14, n.s.) of the
younger families. Thus, the dependence of the elderly on public
services does appear to make them more sensitive to these improvements. They are not, however, necessarily more sensitive to
other types of neighborhood changes. Perhaps they are out in the
neighborhood less than younger individuals.

C. Were "needy" elderly subgroups helped or hurt by revitaliza-tion?

This section is based on analyses of elderly families who remained between waves 1 and 3. Consequently, the sample sizes
for the tables are small, and it is virtually impossible to obtain
statistically significant results. In order to fully utilize the data, we
discuss differences which, while not statistically significant, are
large and meaningful. Because of the small sample sizes, the
results should be treated cautiously.

Although there were considerable attitudinal shifts between

waves 1 and 3, chronological age had little bearing on the likelihood of experiencing such shifts. It is possible, however, that revitalization helped or hurt particular segments of the elderly population. With this possibility in mind, we sought to discover whether, in the UHD experience, revitalization helped or hurt the more "needy" subgroups within the elderly population. There is no support for the belief that the more dependent groups would be most likely to be hurt by revitalization. In fact, revitalization seems to have benefited the low-income elderly (below $7000) in terms of perceived improvements in public services (73 percent, 15 versus 22 percent, 9, for higher income families). The lower income elderly also were less likely to experience increases in their housing cost burden (40 percent, 15, versus 57 percent, 14, higher income families).

In addition, the results of our analysis provide no support for our hypothesis that rising costs would be a particularly severe problem for elderly renters. In fact, a larger proportion of elderly owners than renters experienced a large increase in their housing cost burden during this period (46 percent, 44, versus 38 percent, 8, n.s.). Revitalization appears to have benefited another "needy" group, the "old-old." Those over eighty were more likely to perceive a reduction in the crime problem and also were more likely to perceive an improvement in the neighborhood as a place to make friends.

Neighborhood improvement had a mixed impact on a third dependent group comprised of widows, widowers, and those never married. These individuals were particularly likely to raise their rating of the neighborhood as a good place for making friends, but, on the other hand, they were less likely to perceive a decline in crime than were married couples. Population shifts in the UHD neighborhoods appear to have hurt the black elderly (sometimes viewed as a dependent group in the elderly population). Among householders changing their rating of their neighborhood for making friends, the black elderly were more likely to perceive their neighborhood as a worse place for making friends (33 percent, 27, versus 11 percent, 64, p < .02). This finding may reflect a growing lower-class population and an increasing crime problem in some of the predominantly black UHD neighborhoods, which made it difficult for the black elderly to maintain familiar social patterns and contacts.

Conclusions

By focusing on the experiences of residents of the Urban Homesteading Demonstration neighborhoods, this chapter has provided some of the first empirical evidence on the experiences of the elderly during the course of a neighborhood revitalization program. The results at the start of the Demonstration refute some prevalent stereotypes of the elderly in declining inner-city neighborhoods. Specifically, there is no evidence that the elderly were more likely than younger families to have a higher housing cost burden, to live in deteriorating housing, or to be particularly susceptible to street crime. On the other hand, the results support two other widely accepted assumptions about the elderly: they are overhoused, and they are less likely to invest in housing improvements and repairs.

The results provide little support for the concerns of some writers that revitalization programs hurt the elderly through rising housing costs and shattered social patterns. Over the course of the Demonstration, the elderly did not become more likely to perceive increases in rental costs or in property taxes; nor did they become more likely to anticipate increases in these costs. Even in areas with the most obvious signs of revitalization, the elderly were not more likely to experience increased housing cost burdens or decreased levels of social participation. Furthermore, the results reveal no consistent pattern to suggest that even the most needy subgroups within the elderly population were hurt by revitalization.

Chapter 9

The Prospects For Neighborhood Upgrading

This monograph has examined the ability of the Urban Homesteading Demonstration to stabilize the populations and improve housing conditions in about forty neighborhoods across the United States. We began the evaluation by comparing population changes in selected UHD neighborhoods with control areas, but, recognizing the inherent weaknesses of this type of aggregate analysis, we expanded the analysis to examine the impact of Urban Homesteading on individual households. It was assumed that those living on homesteading blocks would be more aware of rehabilitation activity and that this awareness would lead to greater optimism about the future of the neighborhood, which would result in the decision to remain and invest in property improvements.

In contradiction to the early hopes and expectations about the effects of homesteading, the UHD neighborhoods did not experience improvements relative to the controls in income level and did not experience lower rates of racial change. These insignificant impacts were paralleled at the household level. Living on a homesteading block did not lead to higher confidence levels, to decisions to remain at the location, or to higher repair expenditures.

Conversely, fears about the program having adverse impacts on needy subgroups like the elderly were exaggerated. Even in UHD neighborhoods experiencing the most obvious signs of revitalization, the elderly did not experience disproportionately large increases in housing costs or shattered social patterns.

Why has Urban Homesteading been such a failure in promoting revitalization? It might be argued that the Demonstration was concluded too quickly to detect improvements. There is, unfortunately, no basis for speculating how much longer this expensive study would have had to be extended to test conclusively for neighborhood spillover effects. Alternatively, it is likely that the density of homesteading properties in particular neighborhoods was too low (usually about 1 percent of the total housing stock) to affect investment and/or mobility behavior in the broader area. The lack of impact for the homesteading proximity variable may have been due to the fact that typically no more than one property per block was involved in this program. Clearly, there is a need for future studies of revitalization programs to include measures of the density of rehabilitation activity.

A third explanation for the insignificant impacts also seems more tenable. Many of the UHD neighborhoods were experiencing significant racial and income changes during the 1970s (Chapters 3 and 4). The Demonstration was too narrowly focused on housing and other physical improvements to achieve demographic stabilization and to insure that the housing improvements were maintained over time.

Chapters 5 through 7 highlighted socioeconomic shifts as an obstacle to revitalization. Concerns about racial and income change, as well as low neighborhood ratings for childrearing and property upkeep, played a key role in contributing to neighborhood pessimism, decisions to move, and to low repair expenditures. Leven et al. (1976), using a different methodology, reached a similar conclusion for St. Louis. In contrast, neighborhood physical problems played a far more minor role in affecting neighborhood confidence and mobility/investment behavior.

Program planners appear to have ignored demographic shifts that occurred in many of the UHD communities. Wynnefield and Mt. Airy (Philadelphia) are probably fairly representative. In these communities, the neighborhood conservation component of homesteading was limited to a small voucher program for the distribution of supplies of paints and brushes to enable residents to improve their homes. Obviously, this type of cosmetic program cannot begin to influence population shifts.

Even if the neighborhood preservation component had been expanded in the forty UHD neighborhoods, this probably would not have made that much difference, since localistic programs are inherently limited in their ability to affect community decline. Assessments of public programs in general, and neighborhood public schools in particular, had little impact on confidence levels and on both repair and mobility decisions. Consequently, improvements in these services would not have had that much effect.

Community organizing is also of limited benefit in promoting revitalization in racially/economically changing communities. Improved communications among neighbors is desirable in itself but is unlikely to allay fears, since they are formed from accurate perceptions of what is occurring in nearby communities and from realistic assessments of what is likely to occur in the neighborhood in the near future. In other words, residents are usually aware of and sensitive to ghetto expansion patterns. The fact that concerns about neighborhood quality for childrearing and about property upkeep were influential among blacks and whites refutes the notion that these worries were simply a product of racial stereotyping.

Finally, there is little basis for optimism about local government's ability (either through organizing or other means) to allay the above concerns, i.e., to create "good neighborhoods" where residents would be willing to watch and protect neighbors' children on local streets, and where they would be willing to pressure others to maintain their properties adequately. In white ethnic neighborhoods, usually mentioned to illustrate "viability," surveillance and peer pressure flow naturally from a common nationality background and shared interests. It would be inappropriate for government to try to promote this type of homogeneity. On the other hand, there have been few documented examples of the introduction of these desirable social patterns by government agencies into lower class or ethnically changing areas.

Thus, the prospects for localistic neighborhood revitalization programs like Urban Homesteading vary considerably by com-

munity type. They are poor in racially changing areas because of
the tendency for these communities to experience income/social
class succession following racial change. Increases in the proportion of lower class families is accompanied not only by a decline in
housing conditions but also by serious social problems, including,
but not limited to, violent street crime. Eventually, the process of
decline reaches the point where the community is no longer
viable or capable of achieving upgrading (Chapter 1). The best
ways to improve the prospects for neighborhood revitalization in
this type of community would be to reduce poverty while, at the
same time, deconcentrating the poor. Downs (1981, p. 124) indicates that the first goal could be promoted

> . . . through national monetary policies designed to achieve high
> levels of employment, special incentives to encourage the hiring
> of structurally unemployable persons (those whose lack of skills
> keeps them without jobs even during normal prosperity
> periods) and tax and transfer payment policies that redistribute
> income to the poor, especially those who cannot work.

Policies to raise achievement levels in inner-city schools and to
reduce the incidence of female-headed households would also be
critically important in reducing poverty levels. It is beyond the intended scope of this book to provide a detailed discussion of these
antipoverty strategies.

The prospects for successful upgrading in this type of community would also be dependent on implementing metropolitan
housing policies aimed at deconcentrating low- and moderate-
income families, many of whom are black. A key factor fostering
existing patterns of racial and income change is the concentration
of middle-income black demand on white communities adjoining
the ghetto; and later, for lower income black demand to be focused on newly integrated areas. Housing dispersal policies would
help to slow this process of change by reducing black demand for
housing in these areas. Consequently, white residents would be
more confident about these areas remaining racially mixed,
rather than becoming predominantly black. Furthermore, even if
it were not possible to achieve stable racial integration, the prospects for stabilizing these communities as middle-income black
would be improved. That is, with such dispersal policies in place,

middle-income blacks would be less fearful about their neighborhood, including the local school losing its middle-income character.

One approach to deconcentrating the poor is to increase the amount of government subsidized housing outside the central city. However, federally subsidized housing programs have been cut back sharply in recent years, and it is unlikely that state programs will make up for the loss. A more promising approach is the federal government's housing allowance program, which provides money to owners or renters who then locate adequate units. When the U.S. Department of Housing and Urban Development's Experimental Housing and Urban Development's Experimental Housing Allowance Program (EHAP) was instituted, it was hoped that it would reduce patterns of racial and economic segregation. Frieden (1980, p. 28) notes that this occurred to a limited degree only. "For those (allowance participants) who did move, the program did not improve access to the suburbs, but it did help them to move to better and less segregated neighborhoods in the cities." Thus, if the housing allowance program is to have a greater deconcentrating effect, it will be necessary to not only enforce antidiscrimination statutes but also to provide counseling and other types of help to prospective movers.

Ideally, metropolitan-wide housing policies would be implemented with metropolitan-wide school districts. In the past, efforts to desegregate central city school districts have been counterproductive, leading to the further outmigration of whites and middle-income families. Metropolitan school desegregation would assure citizens that schools would be integrated no matter where they lived. Unfortunately, progress toward both metropolitan housing and school desegregation has been slow. Dayton and Minneapolis-St. Paul are unique in having metropolitan housing plans that have been implemented to a significant degree. Louisville's school desegregation plan is unusual not only for encompassing the suburbs but also for exempting integrated neighborhoods from busing, a rare example of the coordination of housing and school policies (Orfield, 1981).

One reason why there has been such limited progress in implementing these metropolitan policies is that so few citizens (low- or middle-income, black or white) support them. It would be in the interest of neighborhood organizations (e.g., churches and synagogues) concerned with neighborhood upgrading to support such metropolitan housing and educational policies.

It has always been easier to achieve successful upgrading in stable, predominantly white areas, since there the program would focus on the attainable goal of reducing physical deterioration without having to deal with the intractable problem of demographic stabilization. Furthermore, programs directed at this limited physical deterioration (e.g., block beautification efforts) could be used to further strengthen *already sound* social fabrics by bringing residents together around common efforts.

The preceding suggests a serious dilemma for policymakers attempting to allocate limited housing rehabilitation funds. Efficiency criteria would favor allocations to white ethnic communities where housing improvements would more likely succeed and be maintained over time. Housing rehabilitation would have greater spillover effects, as long as it was sufficiently concentrated (Chapter Seven). On the other hand, equity criteria would favor ethnically changing and predominantly black communities, since the social needs would be greater because these areas are often economically discriminated against by banks and other private institutions and because help is needed to sustain the quality of life for residents in the face of decline. No attempt will be made here to resolve this difficult policy dilemma.

Up to this point, the chapter has painted a fairly bleak picture regarding the UHD program and the prospects for neighborhood revitalization programs in general because of the difficulties of counteracting the adverse effects of neighborhood demographic changes. But perhaps the picture need not be quite so gloomy. Many of the racially changing communities currently targeted for revitalization programs are attractive suburban-type areas with high rates of owner occupancy. Others are inner-city ones experiencing middle-class inmigration but not necessarily complete gentrification. Additional research is needed on the prospects for achieving revitalization in such divergent areas. More specifically, answers must be sought to the following five questions.

1. How effective are some of the innovative racial stabilization policies being implemented by suburban governments such as Oak Park's (Illinois) Housing Counseling Program? Under what

circumstances are these programs suitable for central cities? As noted earlier, these programs have a greater potential for success than earlier efforts because they have the full backing of local government and because they focus directly on the local housing market.

2. To what degree is Clay's assertion, that certain types of racially changing communities (e.g., with few multiunit structures) have better upgrading prospects, valid? If it is valid, then programs like Urban Homesteading and Neighborhood Housing Service might be targeted to those racially changing areas with the best prospects for success. Although this type of "triage" would be highly controversial, the approach might be necessary to have some successful examples of revitalization in ethnically mixed and changing areas. Additional research on the mobility decisions of middle-class blacks in racially changing communities would be helpful in assessing the feasibility of successful revitalization in this type of community.

3. What are the long-term effects of strategies like the Neighborhood Housing Service and Urban Homesteading? As indicated, the insignificant impacts for Urban Homesteading might reflect the short time the program had been in operation, and research over a longer time period may detect meaningful impacts. Better data is needed on the influence of different program components (e.g., citizen participation, code enforcement, improvements in public services).

It is unlikely that the federal government will fund sophisticated, expensive research like the NHS, UHD and CDBG studies in the near future. It is therefore important for cities to assume the responsibility for monitoring changes in these neighborhoods and to utilize a variety of available data sources beyond that of the census, including data collected annually in many cities by R.K. Polk Company (see Goetze, 1980). Furthermore, it is important to combine detailed statistical analyses with qualitative research, such as that done by Schoenberg and Rosenbaum for St. Louis. Only in this way will it be possible to determine whether programs like the UHD and NHS help to enhance the social viability of these areas.

4. What types of policies are most likely to be effective in attracting middle-income families to declining communities? To

date, most of the emphasis in stabilization programs has been on "holding" existing middle-income families. Over time, stability is dependent upon attracting new middle-income families to replace those relocating as a result of normal turnover. Until now, there has been little research on factors affecting the willingness to move into such neighborhoods. Answers to this question could be sought through metropolitan-wide surveys asking respondents why they did or did not consider particular areas and what types of changes might have been necessary for them to consider central-city locations seriously.

5. What is the relation between gentrification and upgrading? Is it true, as is commonly believed, that once gentrification begins, it inevitably leads to replacement of the existing population? Or is it possible, as some of the studies in Chapter One suggest, that the two processes may sometimes overlap (that is, the inmigration of middle-class families make existing families more optimistic about the neighborhood, thereby causing them to invest in their own properties). A number of programs have been proposed to achieve the goal of helping both groups, such as programs to attract middle-income families to the local public schools, and to make renters into homeowners. Pilot studies of such efforts are urgently needed.

In conclusion, three implications of this study for housing and neighborhood preservation policy should be stressed. First, policymakers should not overestimate the spillover effects of housing rehabilitation programs. The UHD program involved highly visible housing improvements but had negligible effects on neighbors. It would only be realistic to anticipate spillover effects where the housing improvements are *both* visible and concentrated. In those favorable circumstances, the spillovers would only extend to neighbors on the same block and would influence repair but not necessarily mobility decisions.

Second, in justifying subsidized housing rehabilitation programs (grants, as well as loans) housing advocates should rely primarily on the direct benefits to participants, which are well substantiated (as in the UHD), rather than the indirect benefits, which are not.

Finally, policymakers, bankers, community leaders and residents need to be more realistic and candid about the pros-

pects for reversing patterns of decline in demographically changing areas along the boundaries of expanding central-city ghettos.
The assertion in the *President's National Urban Policy Report* (1984),
that *all* types of communities can achieve "incumbent upgrading"
through community organization and the catalytic efforts of
private institutions and civic groups, is inaccurate and diverts attention from the more complex and difficult problems (poverty,
racial discrimination) that will have to be solved to make
revitalization a real possibility in all parts of the city.

Appendix Table 1. Variables included in regression analysis

Variable	
Repair activity	Total amount spent on repairs 1977/1978, plus total amount spent 1978/1979.
Residential mobility	Amount of time remained at location after the 1977 interview: (1) below 1 year, (2) 1 year to less than 2 years, (3) 2 years or more.
Neighborhood confidence	(1) pessimistic (e.g. neighborhood poor and expected to get worse) or neither pessimistic or optimistic (i.e., neighborhood "so-so" and expected to remain that way), (2) optimistic (e.g., neighborhood good and expected to get better).
Housing satisfaction	Condition of house as a whole: (0) poor, "so-so"; (1) good.
Highest grade	Household head, answers ranged from 0 to 21.
Employed	(0) not employed, (1) employed.
Skilled worker	(0) other, (1) skilled worker.
Unskilled worker	(0) other, (1) unskilled worker.
Professional worker	(0) other, (1) professional worker.
Income	Total family income from all sources, 10 categories.
Welfare	(0) do not receive, (1) receive.
Black	(0) nonblack, (1) black or black Hispanic.
Age	Age of household head.

Variable	
Children below 18	(0) none, (1) one or more.
Female household head	(0) no, (1) yes.
Owner	(0) other, (1) owner.
Length of residence at location	
Homesteading block	(0) one or more blocks away, (1) same block.
Whether white/neighborhood below 25% black	(0) no, (1) yes, racial composition from 1977 survey.
Whether white/neighborhood 25–49% black	(0), no, (1) yes, racial composition from 1977 survey.
Whether white/neighborhood 50–74% black	(0) no, (1) yes, racial composition from 1977 survey.
Whether high-income family/ low-income neighborhood	(0) no, (1) yes, neighborhood income from 1977 survey.
Whether high-income family/ high-income neighborhood	(0) no, (1) yes, neighborhood income from 1977 survey.
Whether low-income family/ high-income neighborhood	(0) no, (1) yes, neighborhood income from 1977 survey.
Proportion of neighborhood homes 40 or more years old	From 1977 UHD neighborhood residents survey.
Poor block conditions	Factor score based on rating of streets, sidewalks and curbs from 1977 windshield survey, high scores indicate poor conditions.
Poor housing conditions	Factor score based on rating of quality of exterior paint and trim and general condition of structures from 1977 windshield survey, high scores indicate poor conditions.

Variable	
Neighborhood proportion black	From 1977 UHD neighborhood residents survey.
Neighborhood income level	From 1977 UHD neighborhood residents survey.
Neighborhood proportion owners	From 1977 UHD neighborhood residents survey.
Neighborhood proportion long-term residents	Percentage of residents living at location 10 years or more.
Neighborhood repair activity	Neighborhood mean property repairs, from 1979 UHD neighborhood residents survey
Change in repair activity	Mean investment level 1979/mean investment level 1977.
Property values	Mean property values 1977 from UHD neighborhood residents survey.
Change in property values	Mean property values, 1979/mean property values, 1977.
Change proportion black	Neighborhood proportion black, 1980—neighborhood proportion black, 1970, federal censuses.
Whether high neighborhood income/good housing conditions	Neighborhood income from 1977 UHD residents survey, housing conditions from 1977 windshield survey.
Whether high neighborhood income/poor housing conditions	Neighborhood income from 1977 UHD residents survey, housing conditions from 1977 windshield survey.
Whether low neighborhood income/poor housing conditions	Neighborhood income from 1977 UHD residents survey, housing conditions from 1977 windshield survey.

Variable	
Whether concerned about housing abandonment	Based on 2 items, whether aware of condition, and whether concerned.
Whether concerned about income changes	Based on 2 items, whether aware of condition, and whether concerned.
Whether concerned about racial changes	Based on 2 items, whether aware of condition, and whether concerned.
Poor property maintenance	Four categories, ranging from all neighbors try to keep up to few try.
Neighborhood problems	Whether dissatisfied with one or more of the following (street noise, traffic, roads, lights, litter, abandoned houses, crime).
Neighborhood poor for friendships	(0) "so-so" or good, (1) poor.
Neighborhood poor for childrearing	(0) "so-so" or good, (1) poor
Public service problems	Whether dissatisfied with one or more of the following (public transit, neighborhood shopping, police protection, parks-recreation, garbage collection.
Concern about neighborhood public schools	Based on two items: whether public schools very important in moving decision, and whether local public schools considered worse than others in city.
Neighborhood social cohesiveness	Scores 0–2. Count of whether neighbors were very friendly, and whether it was very easy to recognize a stranger.

Variable	
Level of social interaction	Scores 0–2. Count of whether respondent met with neighbors at least several times a week, and whether he/she know most/all neighbors.
Cost burden	Total housing costs (mortgage or rent, plus utilities) divided by total family income.
Number of rooms	Total in the house: bathrooms, porches, balconies, foyers and half rooms were not included.
Housing density	Household size divided by total number of rooms.
Age of house	Five categories ranging from 3 to 50 years or more.
Property tax rate	Estimate of property tax divided by estimate of property value.
Housing defects	Whether any of the following aspects of the house were "so-so" or poor: walls, ceilings and floors; the heating system; the plumbing system; the electrical system; the roof; the exterior painting or siding.
Wooden construction	(0) other, (1) wood.
Multiunit structure	(0) owner of single family home, (1) resident owner in multiunit structure
Repairs previous year	total repair costs, 1976–1977.

Appendix Table 2. Comparison of means for regression sample remaining between 1977 and 1979, and for total sample

Characteristic	Sample remaining N=650	Total sample N = 1675
Neighborhood housing poor (factor score)	-.04	-.02
Block conditions poor (factor score)	-.03	-.01
Proportion of old buildings	.46	.47
Neighborhood proportion black	62.90	63.34
Neighborhood income level	10875.11	10810.60
Neighborhood proportion owners	69.14	68.93
Mean repair expenditures	1058.80	1077.97
Mean, change in repair expenditures	208.55	250.01
Change in neighborhood property values	100.64	101.71
Change in neighborhood proportion black	18.77	19.21
Neighborhood property values	20728.40	20678.13
Highest grade	10.88	10.98
Family income	11497.41	10778.08
Age	48.95	47.24
Length of residence	11.46	10.36

Appendix Table 3. Comparison of means for three regression samples: confidence, mobility and repairs

Characteristic	Regression sample, confidence N = 273	Regression sample mobility N = 199	Regression sample repairs N = 192
Neighborhood housing poor (factor score)	-.03	-.05	-.06
Block conditions poor (factor score)	-.01	-.08	-.07
Proportion of old buildings	.43	.43	.43
Neighborhood proportion black	63.59	58.62	—
Neighborhood income level	11121.54	—	—
Neighborhood proportion owners	70.19	71.07	69.96
Mean repair expenditures	960.53	703.30	690.43
Mean, change in repair expenditures	201.88	202.99	—
Change in neighborhood property values	98.63	101.95	—
Change in neighborhood proportion black	19.97	18.34	—
Neighborhood property values	21341.56	22032.70	22621.88
Highest grade	11.37	11.21	11.81
Family income	13021.98	14095.48	—
Age	45.79	46.03	43.32
Length of residence	9.75	10.78	10.51

Note: Blanks are inserted above for variables not included in the regression equation.

Notes

Chapter One

1. Neighborhood revitalization is a broader term encompassing both upgrading and gentrification. The former refers to physical improvement with the existing population remaining in place. The latter applies to community improvements resulting from the replacement of a working/lower class population by a middle-class one. It is beyond the intended scope of this chapter to review the now extensive literature on gentrification (see Gale, 1984; Schill and Nathan, 1983). We do however discuss gentrification when it occurs alongside upgrading in the same community and where gentrification affects the prospects for successful upgrading.

2. The classic models of land use (e.g., concentric zones, sectors) developed by human ecologists provide similar explanations of neighborhood decline (see, for example, Herbert, 1972, p. 70–78).

3. Although neighborhood decline is linked with racial change, this does not mean that the black community should be blamed for this decline. To the contrary, white racism is the fundamental cause of such problems as poverty and racial segregation which contribute to social class and racial change. Nevertheless, there is increasing recognition of the desirability of black leaders assuming some of the responsibility for solving such problems as criminality among young blacks and the precipitous rise in female-headed households, two problems which undermine the viability of black neighborhoods. As Loury (1985, p. 11) notes:

> It is absolutely vital that blacks distinguish between the fault which may be attributed to racism as a cause of the black condition and the respon-

sibility for relieving that condition. For no people can be genuinely free so long as they look to others for their deliverance.

William Raspberry (1985), a black journalist, makes essentially the same point.

4. Some researchers assert that crime is not a serious problem in racially changing communities. Clay (1979) sees the crime problem as a result of the conflict between generations, "between the impetuousness of youth and the fearfulness of old age," implying that elderly whites often exaggerate the seriousness of the problem. Similarly, Wireman (1984) criticizes whites for overreacting to the cocky street behavior of black teenagers and warns against restricting teenage movements (e.g., curfews, limits on the number who can enter a store at one time). Both Clay and Wireman overlook the legitimate concerns of residents and shopkeepers (e.g., loitering, vandalism) well documented in the case studies of racially changing communities.

5. Columbia, Maryland, and Reston, Virginia, are two notable examples of successful, planned, integrated communities (Wireman, 1984). But their stability results from their distance from any sizable black ghetto. See Bradburn, Sudman and Gockel (1971) for an extended discussion of the meaning and measurement of stable racial integration.

6. This is no coincidence. Since these suburban localities are predominantly middle-income, they can focus on the problem of racial stabilization, whereas central cities are so preoccupied with poverty related problems (e.g., welfare) that racial stabilization is usually given low priority.

7. Jewish federations are the main fund raising and planning bodies for the Jewish communities in individual metropolitan areas. They are roughly equivalent to Community Chests and United Ways which serve the total community.

8. Advocates of housing programs have sometimes cited the existence of broader societal benefits, such as economic stimulation and reduced unemployment. See Varady (1982) for a discussion of these broader benefits. They are not discussed here because they are more appropriate for new housing than housing rehabilitation programs.

Chapter Two

1. This section on rural homesteading programs draws from USR&E, 1977b, Volume 3, p. 13–32.

2. The twenty-three cities were: Atlanta, Baltimore, Boston, Chicago, Cincinnati, Columbus, Dallas, Decatur (Georgia), Freeport (New York), Gary, Indianapolis, Islip (New York), Jersey City, Kansas City, Milwaukee, Minneapolis, New York, Oakland, Philadelphia, Rockford (Illinois), South Bend (Indiana), Tacoma, and Wilmington.

3. For additional information on the UHD homesteader and neighborhood residents surveys, see Blackburn (1980) and Pedone, Remch and Case, 1980.

4. See USR&E, 1977a, p. 56. Such large subareas as the Northwest Side are more accurately described as sectors than neighborhoods (Broden et al., 1980). It was a mistake for HUD to allow cities to consider sectors as neighborhoods because statistics for the former obscured the diversity at lower levels of aggregation.

5. Chapter One discussed the reasons for this noninvolvement.

6. The UHD neighborhood residents data set includes measures of householder perceptions and evaluations of racial and race-related shifts. Pedone, Remch and Case. (1980, p. 142) excluded racial change from USR&E's mobility analysis to make the results comparable to those from an earlier report by Schnare (1979).

Chapter Three

1. The choice of race, income and tenant status as the indicators of population change can certainly be questioned. Such a challenge would not be surprising because there is a lack of consensus among scholars concerning measures of community change. For example, whereas Hughes and Bleakly (1975) view an increase in minorities as an indicator of decline, Ahlbrandt and Brophy (1975) argue that racial transition does not signify decline unless it is closely associated with a drop in income levels.

A rise in the average income level is desirable in that it indicates an increased ability among residents to afford housing repairs. However, too rapid a rise in income could signify gentrification and possibly the displacement of lower income residents.

An increase in the proportion of renters has often been used as an indication of community deterioration since the rise may reflect the conversion of single family units to apartments. Although such conversions are sometimes accompanied by declines in housing quality, this does not necessarily have to be the case. The conversions may reflect a tight housing market and high levels of demand among young professional singles and couples. This conclusion is supported by detailed analyses of socioeconomic and housing changes in eight of the UHD neighborhoods in five cities (Varady and Torok, 1984). Tacoma's three UHD neighborhoods were the only ones to experience declines in the proportions of owners, with one neighborhood experiencing a 12 percent drop. Nevertheless, these three did far better than the five others with respect to almost all of the other indicators of improvement such as property values, contract rent and family income. Thus, increases in the proportion of renters may not always indicate community decline.

Although there are problems with each of the three community change indicators used, it is unlikely, however, that had different variables been used the results would have been very different.

2. The boundaries of the UHD neighborhoods in this chapter differ from the neighborhood boundaries in the original USR&E study. When city officials selected the UHD neighborhoods, the boundaries cut through census tracts. Thus, a UHD neighborhood might consist of 100 percent of tract A, 80 percent of tract B and 40 percent of tract C. In order to take advantage of 1970 and 1980 census tract information, we reassembled the UHD neighborhoods by combining whole tracts, even if parts of the tracts were not in the UHD neighborhoods. Combining the whole tracts made the UHD neighborhoods in this analysis larger than those in the original study, which, in turn, made it more difficult to detect neighborhood impacts, since the effects of homesteading are most likely to be apparent in the immediate area of rehabilitation.

We would have liked to recreate the UHD neighborhoods from census blocks, but unfortunately the needed information was unavailable. We considered, but decided against, weighting the census tract data to reflect the proportion of particular tracts in the UHD neighborhoods. This would have greatly added to the complexity of the analysis, without changing the results very much.

Chapter Four

1. This chapter draws upon several earlier studies of Wynnefield by the author (Varady, 1971; Varady, 1979; Varady, forthcoming).

2. This section on Wynnefield's UHD program draws heavily from USR&E, 1977, volume 3.

3. This conclusion is based, in part, on Molotch's 1972 South Shore (Chicago) study in which he notes that white evaluations of crime were based on historical trends. That is, whites were particularly concerned because they were used to living in a community where such incidents

rarely if ever occurred. It follows that black householders' evaluations would be based on the types of communities in which they had previously resided.

Chapter Five

1. The UHD data set includes a measure of the respondent's proximity to the nearest homesteading property, but it does not include a measure of awareness of homesteading as a government-sponsored program. Nevertheless, it seemed reasonable to assume that those living closest would be most likely to be aware of the activity.

2. Preliminary crosstabular analysis of the determinants of confidence revealed that the confidence index did not approximate interval level data and was therefore unsuitable for the regression analysis. On the basis of these results the confidence variable was recoded into two categories: (1) "not optimistic" (pessimistic and neither pessimistic nor optimistic), and (2) optimistic.

Some readers may criticize our use of ordinary least squares regression with a dependent variable. We use OLS rather than PROBIT or LOGIT because results from the former are easier to interpret and more suitable for path diagrams. Further, it is highly unlikely that the conclusions would have differed had a technique like LOGIT been used. Cohen and Cohen (1975, p. 230) defend the use of OLS regression with dichotomous dependent variables.

> It should be noted that dichotomous dependent variables . . . may be coded 1–0 and used as dependent variables. This practice is in formal violation of the model. Yet in practice and with support from the central limit theorem and empirical studies, dichotomous dependent variables are profitably employed in MRC (multiple regression correlation).

We were sensitive to the issue of multicollinearity in the analyses for this and later chapters. If a number of independent variables are highly intercorrelated, this leads to unreliable and fluctuating partial regression coefficients. In order to minimize this problem, we inspected the bivariate correlation matrices, and, where there was extreme collinearity (i.e., in the .8 to 1.0 range), one of the variables in the correlated set was excluded from the regression runs.

3. Originally, we hoped to limit the analysis to cases where the same respondent completed the survey at both points in time. Unfortunately,

to have done so would have reduced the sample available for the regression analysis below acceptable levels.

Appendix Tables 2 and 3 indicate that the sample used for the regression analysis did not differ meaningfully from the sample participating in the two surveys or from the UHD sample as a whole in 1977.

4. Originally, we thought that the statistically insignificant beta between confidence and concerns about racial change might be attributable to the close intercorrelation between the latter variable and the concern about income change. As a result, the latter variable might have served as a proxy for the former in the analysis. Additional regression runs not presented here, limited to only one type of concern, provided no support for this assumption. While the concern about income change had a strong impact on confidence, the concern about racial change did not.

5. The strong direct positive impact of the proportion of blacks in the neighborhood on confidence apparently reflects the optimism of blacks in nearly all black communities. It would have been desirable to know whether these blacks lived in neighborhoods that were historically black or in ones that had recently undergone racial change. On the basis of previous research, the optimism of blacks in historically black areas apart from the ghetto is understandable (e.g., relatively low turnover, strong institutions). It would be more difficult to account for this optimism in areas that had undergone racial turnover, since these areas often experience declines in social and housing conditions.

6. One might argue that black, as well as white, householders were guilty of racial stereotyping if they associated racial shifts with income decline. This argument is not persuasive. There is considerable social science research (see, for example, Leven et al., 1976) documenting the fact that middle-income blacks are often succeeded by lower income ones in racially changing communities.

7. One other result should be noted, even though the variable was not powerful enough to be included in the path diagram. As shown in Table 5.2, the perception that neighbors did not maintain properties contributed to pessimism. Since a high level of upkeep is a good indicator of neighborhood cohesion (Schoenberg and Rosenbaum, 1980), this finding, together with that of childrearing adequacy, confirms the importance of the social fabric in explaining confidence levels.

8. Initially, it seemed surprising that the 1977 school evaluation was a stronger predictor than the 1979 one. However, additional analyses not presented here suggest that the finding resulted from an

unavoidable miscoding of the index measuring concern about local public schools. Families without school age children were not asked the two questions making up the index but were coded "not concerned." To have excluded these families because of missing values would have reduced the sample size below acceptable limits. There were a number of families who were asked these questions in 1977 but not in 1979 because of the maturation of their school age children. The correlation between 1977 concern and pessimism among these families probably reflected their continuing worry that poor quality neighborhood schools would deter middle-income families from moving into the area.

9. Chapter Eight explores in more detail the impact of neighborhood upgrading on the elderly.

Chapter Six

1. A much-criticized feature of the Speare model is the assumption that background characteristics affect mobility only through dissatisfaction. MacMillan's model overcomes this problem by assuming that background characteristics affect mobility directly, as well as indirectly.

2. Economists such as Quigley and Weinberg (1977) have developed residential mobility models comparable to the one used here by equating housing dissatisfaction with a loss in household utility from residing in nonoptimal housing. "The utility loss is termed disequilibrium in housing consumption and approximated by the deviation of current from equilibrium housing consumption" (Onaka, 1983, p. 751). These economic models, while seemingly more sophisticated than the one used by MacMillan, have not resulted in improved predictive ability. Two additional factors contributed to our decision to use a sociological/geographic model rather than an economic one. First, the latter require more precise information on individual households than is usually available. Second, economic models make the unrealistic assumption that all of the variables in the mobility decision are financial.

3. The reader may note differences in the determinants of neighborhood confidence between the last chapter and this one. The dissimilar results are due to the different samples used. Chapter Five was based on the approximately 650 households who remained between 1977 and 1979. This chapter is based on the 390 families who were interviewed in 1977 and for whom mobility and full background data were available for the 1977 to 1979 period.

4. Earlier regression runs included a Likert-type scale measuring the number of aspects of the home perceived as inadequate (e.g., heating system, roof). Since the scale was highly intercorrelated with the overall level of satisfaction with the home, it was not included in the regression runs for this chapter.

Chapter Seven

1. Pedone's research strategy is equally, if not more, problematic than ours. Her investment analysis primarily used wave 3 data. Households were asked about their investment behavior during the twelve months prior to the interview, and both subjective and objective household information was drawn from the third wave. She utilized these postinvestment conditions to explain investment behavior which had already taken place. This approach violates the maxim that the causes should have occurred before the presumed effects. Pedone therefore paid a heavy price for being able to utilize such a large sample in her regression analysis.

We ran a separate set of regressions to determine whether we would have obtained substantively different results by using Pedone's research strategy. Personal and housing characteristics from wave three, along with measures of neighborhood conditions from wave one, were used to predict whether households made any repair expenditures prior to wave three. In fact, the results were quite similar to those discussed in this chapter. Proximity to homesteading had virtually no impact on repair decisions. The two most important predictors of repairs were the perception that neighbors maintained their property and the belief that the neighborhood was a good one for raising children. The concern about racial change decreased the likelihood of making a repair but was less important than the two preceding measures of the quality of the social fabric.

2. Two other versions of the dependent variable were tested: (1) a continuous variable similar to the one used, except that "zeros" were excluded, and (2) a dichotomous variable distinguishing those making major repairs in one or both years from those who did not. The first variable proved unsuitable because it resulted in the reduction of the sample size below acceptable limits. The second proved to be acceptable, but we chose not to include its results because this would have made the chapter overly long and cumbersome. The initial regression results for the dichotomous variable were basically similar to those for the continuous variable used.

3. These insignificant results may also reflect the fact that the neighborhood boundaries used for gathering the statistical information typically encompassed far larger areas than those that were meaningful for the respondents, who were primarily concerned about shifts on their block or in the subneighborhood extending two or three blocks from their home.

4. Alternatively the finding may reflect the fact that racial change occurred in those areas with the most attractive housing.

5. The reader might assume that this variable might serve as a proxy for homesteading activity and might "wash out" the effects of homesteading per se. This was not the case. In separate regression runs, which did not include the concentrated rehabilitation variable, the proximity to homesteading factor continued to play a statistically unimportant role.

Nevertheless, the findings related to the concentrated repair activity variable should be treated cautiously. The correlation between neighborhood and sample rehabilitation activity could be due to the same set of third forces, rather than on a causal relation between neighboring rehabilitation and rehabilitation in the structure examined.

6. The insignificant results may, however, be due to problems with the measures used. No attempt was made to adjust for intermetropolitan housing market variations. For example, a $30,000 average for neighborhood property values may be relatively high in Rockford, Illinois, but would be relatively low in New York City. Had the neighborhood averages and the measures of change been adjusted for what was taking place in the surrounding metropolitan housing markets, the variables might have played more meaningful roles. It was, however, beyond the scope of this book to try to standardize this information.

7. The reader may recall from Chapter Six that unskilled workers were also particularly likely to move. There is no contradiction between the fact and the assertion in this chapter that the unskilled were constrained from moving. The constraints applied to voluntary intrametropolitan moves to improve housing conditions. The moves referred to in Chapter Six were probably unplanned and arose from a desire to find a new or decent-paying job after being laid off. Many of these moves were probably to other cities. The types of housing constraints discussed in this chapter are irrelevant to such "forced" moves.

Skilled workers were the reference category and were not included in the analysis.

8. The initial regression runs also included a measure of household density (family size divided by the number of rooms). Since this index was highly intercorrelated with both family size and the number of rooms, the density measure was excluded from later runs.

9. The regressions for this chapter utilized a continuous type measure of age. A separate regression run (results not presented here) included a dichotomous version (under 65 years, 65 and older), but it, too, proved statistically insignificant.

Chapter Eight

1. The preceding three chapters showed that Urban Homesteading itself was not responsible for improvements, since it did not lead to higher confidence levels among nonparticipating neighbors on homesteading blocks. Nor did it help to hold these residents at their locations and induce them to make property repairs. The question of what caused increased rehabilitation activity in some of the UHD neighborhoods is not a critical one for this chapter. Rather, our interest is on the impacts of increased rehabilitation activity on the elderly, whatever the cause.

2. A major limitation of the UHD data sets is the absence of objective information on the respondent's housing condition, along with the greater tendency for the elderly to provide ambiguous and unreliable responses to questions about their environment (Golant, 1984). Nevertheless, such questions are valuable because they highlight differences within the elderly population and suggest ways to weight different housing problems. Furthermore, the problems of unreliability and ambiguity are less severe with respect to measures of housing conditions than with respect to housing satisfaction (Ferguson et al., undated).

3. The reader may recall from Chapter Seven that age did not play a significant role in explaining repair expenditures. The significant differences in this chapter between the elderly and younger respondents are, therefore, probably attributable to factors associated with age rather than age per se.

References

Ahlbrandt, Roger S., Jr., and Brophy, Paul C. 1975. *Neighborhood Revitalization.* Lexington, Mass.: Lexington Books.

Ahlbrandt, Roger S., Jr., and Cunningham, James V. 1979. *A New Public Policy for Neighborhood Preservation.* New York: Praeger.

Aldrich, Howard. 1975. Ecological Succession in Racially Changing Neighborhoods: A Review of the Literature. *Urban Affairs Quarterly.* 10,3 (March): 327–348.

Armor, David J. 1980. White Flight and the Future of School Desegregation. In *School Desegregation,* edited by Walter G. Staphan and Joe R. Feagin. New York: Plenum Books.

Arthur D. Little, Inc. 1969. *East Cleveland: Response to Urban Change.* Boston: Arthur D. Little, Inc.

Bild, B.R., and Havinghurst, R.J. 1976. Senior citizens in great cities: The case of Chicago. *The Gerontologist.* 16:28–46.

Birch, David L. 1971. Toward a stage theory of urban growth. *Journal of the American Institute of Planners.* 37 (March):78–87.

Blackburn, Anthony J.; Millman, Molly Beals; and Schnare, Ann B. 1981. *Evaluation of the Urban Homesteading Demonstration Project.* Final Report. Volume 1. Summary Assessment. Cambridge, Mass.: Urban Systems, Research and Engineering, Inc.

Blackburn, Anthony J. 1980. *The Rehabilitation of Urban Homesteads.* Cambridge, Mass.: Urban Systems, Research and Engineering, Inc.

Blackburn, Anthony J. 1981. *The Urban Homesteading Demonstration. Final Report. Volume 1.* Cambridge, Mass.: Urban Systems, Research and Engineering, Inc.

Blaine, Edward. 1973. The Community Improvement Program in Jamaica Plain. Master's thesis. Boston University.

Bleakly, Kenneth D.; Holin, Mary Joel; Fitzpatrick, Laura H.; and Newman, Constance. 1982. *The NSA Demonstration: A Case Study of Local Control Over Housing Development.* Cambridge, Mass.: Urban Systems, Research and Engineering, Inc.

Bleakly, Kenneth D.; Holin, Mary Joel; Fitzpatrick, Laura H.; and Hodes, Laurent V. 1983. *A Case Study of Local Control Over Housing Development: The Neighborhood Strategy Area Demonstration.* Washington, D.C.: U.S. Department of Housing and Urban Development.

Bradburn, Norman; Sudman, Seymour; and Gockel, Galen. 1971. *Side by Side: Integrated Neighborhoods in America.* Chicago: Quadrangle Books.

Bratt, Rachell, G. 1983. People and Their Neighborhoods: Attitudes and Policy Implications. In P. Clay and R. Hollister, eds., *Neighborhood Policy and Planning.* Lexington, Mass.: Lexington Books.

Broden, Thomas; Kirkwood, Ronn B.; Roos, John and Swartz, Thomas. 1980. *Neighborhood Identification: A Guide for Participation in the U.S. Census Neighborhood Statistics Program.* Washington, D.C.: U.S. Department of Housing and Urban Development.

Cantor, M. 1973. *Life Space and the Social Support System of the Inner City Elderly of New York.* New York: Office of Aging.

Carp, F.M. 1976. Housing and living environments of older people. In R. Binstock and E. Shanda, eds., *Handbook of Aging and Social Sciences.* New York: Van Nostrand Reinhold Co.

Clay, Phillip. 1979. *Neighborhood Renewal: Middle Class Resettlement and Incumbent Upgrading in American Neighborhoods.* Lexington, Mass.: D.C. Heath and Company.

Clay, Philip. 1980. Neighborhood Revitalization: The Experience and Promise. In J. Pynoos et al., eds., *Housing Urban America*, New York: Aldine.

Clay, Phillip. 1983. Urban Reinvestment: Process and Trends. In P. Clay and R. Hollister, editors, *Neighborhood Policy and Planning.* Lexington, Mass.: Lexington Books.

Cohen, Jacob, and Cohen, Patricia. 1975. *Applied Multiple Regression/ Correlation Analysis for the Behavioral Sciences.* Hillsdale, N.J.: Lawrence Erlbaum Associates.

Cox, Kevin R. 1982. Housing tenure and neighborhood activism. *Urban Affairs Quarterly*. 18,1 (September): 107–130.

Dear, M.; Fincher, R.; and Currie, L. 1977. Measuring the External Effects of Public Programs. *Environment and Planning. A*. 9: 137–147.

DeSalvo, J.S. 1974. Neighborhood Upgrading: Effects of Middle Income Projects in New York City. *Journal of Urban Economics*. 1,3: 269–277.

Downs, Anthony. 1968. Alternative Futures for the American Ghetto. *Daedalus* 97,4 (Fall): 1331–1379.

Downs, Anthony. 1980. Using the Lessons of Experience to Allocate Resources in Community Development Programs. In Jon Pynoos, Robert Schaefer, Chester Hartman, eds., *Housing Urban America*. 2nd edition. New York: Aldine.

Downs, Anthony. 1981. *Neighborhoods and Urban Development*. Washington, D.C.: The Brookings Institution.

Ferguson, Gary D.; Holin, Mary Joel; and Moss, William G. Undated. *An Evaluation of the Seven City Home Maintenance Demonstration for the Elderly: Final Report. Volume I*. Cambridge, Mass.: Urban Systems, Research and Engineering, Inc.

Fried, Joseph P. 1976. Housing Abandonment Spreads in Bronx and Parts of Brooklyn. *New York Times*. April 12, 1976.

Frieden, Bernard J. 1980. "Housing Allowances: An Experiment that Worked." *The Public Interest*. 59, 15–35.

Gale, Dennis E. 1984. *Neighborhood Revitalization and the Post Industrial City*. Lexington, Mass.: Lexington Books.

Galster, George, and Hesser, Gary W. 1982. The Social Neighborhood: An Unspecified Factor in Homeowner Maintenance? *Urban Affairs Quarterly*. 18,2 (December): 235–254.

Ginsberg, Ralph B. 1983. *Offsite Effects: Community Development Strategies Evaluation*. Philadelphia: University of Pennsylvania.

Ginsberg, Yona. 1975. *Jews in a Changing Neighborhood: The Study of Mattapan*. New York: Free Press.

Goering, John. 1978. Neighborhood Tipping and Racial Transition: A Review of Social Science Evidence. *Journal of the American Institute of Planners*. 44,1 (January): 68–78.

Goetze, Rolf. 1976. *Building Neighborhood Confidence: A Humanistic Strategy for Urban Housing.* Cambridge, Mass.: Ballinger Publishing Company.

Goetze, Rolf. 1979. *Understanding Neighborhood Change: The Role of Expectations in Urban Revitalization.* Cambridge, Mass.: Ballinger Publishing.

Goetze, Rolf. 1980. *Neighborhood Monitoring and Analysis: A New Way of Looking at Urban Neighborhoods and How they Change.* Washington, D.C.: U.S. Department of Housing and Urban Development.

Goetze, R., and Colton, K. 1983. The Dynamics of Neighborhoods: A Fresh Approach to Understanding Housing and Neighborhood Change. In P. Clay and R. Hollister, *Neighborhood Policy and Planning.* Lexington, Mass.: Lexington Books.

Golant, Stephen, M. 1984. Subjective assessments by the elderly: A critical component in the housing evaluation process. Paper presented to the American Planning Association meeting, Minneapolis, Minn., May 9, 1984.

Goodman, John L., Jr. 1978. *Urban Residential Mobility: places, people and policy.* Washington, D.C.: Urban Institute.

Grigsby, William; Baratz, Morton; and Maclennan, Duncan. 1984. *The Dynamics of Neighborhood Change and Decline.* Research Report Series: No. 4. Philadelphia: Department of City and Regional Planning, University of Pennsylvania.

Grigsby, William G.; White, Sammis B.; Levine, Daniel U.; Kelly, Regina M.; Perelman, Marsha Reines; and Claflen, George L., Jr. 1977. *Rethinking Housing and Community Development Policy.* Philadelphia: University of Pennsylvania, Department of City and Regional Planning.

Herbert, David. 1972. *Urban Geography: A Social Perspective.* New York: Praeger.

Hollister, Robert M., with Deborah Auger, Adrian Ruth Walter and Timothy Pattison. 1978. *Measuring Neighborhood Confidence.* Cambridge, Mass.: Massachusetts Institute of Technology, Department of Urban Studies and Planning.

Hughes, James W., and Bleakly, Kenneth D., Jr. 1975. *Urban Homesteading.* New Brunswick: Rutgers University, Center for Urban Research.

Jewish Community Relations Council of Philadelphia. undated. *Survey of Racial Changes in the Wynnefield Area of Philadelphia.* Philadelphia: JCRC

Jewish Exponent. 1969. Wynnefield is a Neighborhood that is 'Making It.' June 6, 1969.

Jud, G. Donald. 1985. Public Schools and Urban Development. *Journal of the American Planning Association.* 51,1 (Winter): 74–83.

Kain, John F., and Quigley, John M. Measuring the Value of Housing Quality. 1970. *Journal of the American Statistical Association.* 65 (June): 532–546.

Katzman, Martin T. 1983. The Flight of Blacks from Central City Public Schools. *Urban Education.* 18,3 (October): 259–283.

Klausner, Samuel Z., and Varady, David P. 1970. *Synagogues Without Ghettos.* Philadelphia: Center for Research on the Acts of Man.

Kolodny, Robert. 1983. Policy Implications of Theories of Neighborhood Change. In P. Clay and R. Hollister, eds., *Neighborhood Policy and Planning.* Lexington Mass.: Lexington Books.

Lee, Barrett A., and Mergenhagen, Paula M. 1984. Is Revitalization Detectable?: Evidence from 5 Nashville Neighborhoods. *Urban Affairs Quarterly.* 19,4 (June): 511–538.

Lee, Clifton O. 1979. Integration Success: Wynnefield Survives, Prospers as a Community in which Races Exist Together. *Philadelphia Bulletin.* December 9, 1979.

Leven, Charles L.; Little, James T.; Nourse, Hugh O.; and Reed, R. B. 1976. *Neighborhood Change: Lessons in the Dynamics of Urban Decay.* New York: Praeger.

Li, M.M., and Brown, H.J. 1980. Micro-Neighborhood Externalities and Hedonic Housing Prices. *Land Economics.* 56,2 (1980): 125–141.

London, Bruce, and Palen, J. John. 1984. Introduction: Some Theoretical and Practical Issues Regarding Inner City Revitalization. In J.J. Palen and B. London, eds., *Gentrification, Displacement and Neighborhood Revitalization.* Albany, N.Y.: State University of New York Press.

Loury, Glenn C. 1985. The Moral Quandry of the Black Community. *The Public Interest.* 79, Spring: 9–22.

Lowry, Ira S. 1981. *Experimenting with Housing Allowances: The Comprehensive Final Report of the HASE*. Santa Monica, California: Rand Institute.

McCray, Jackie. 1985. Neighborhood Monitoring Systems: A Method for Identifying Change in Cincinnati, Ohio. Bachelors thesis. School of Planning, University of Cincinnati.

McFarland, John. 1984. An Evaluation of Residential Housing Rehabilitation Under the Community Development Block Grant Program in Springfield, Illinois. Student paper. Department of Geography, Western Illinois University.

MacMillan, Jean. 1980. *Mobility in the Housing Allowance Demand Experiment*. Cambridge, Mass.: Abt Associates.

Marans. Robert W., and Rogers, Willard. 1972. *Toward an Understanding of Community Satisfaction*. East Lansing, Michigan: Institute for Social Research, University of Michigan.

Mayer, Neil S. 1984. Conserving Rental Housing: A Policy Analysis. *Journal of the American Planning Association*. 50,3 (Summer): 311–325.

Meier, Ron B. 1983. Code Enforcement and Housing Quality Revisited. *Urban Affairs Quarterly*. 19,2 (December): 255–273.

Mendelsohn, Robert. 1977. Empirical Evidence on Home Improvements. *Journal of Urban Economics*. 4 (October): 459–468.

Molotch, Harvey L. 1972. *Managed Integration: Dilemmas of Doing Good in the City*. Berkeley, California: University of California Press.

Muth, Richard F. 1969. *Cities and Housing*. Chicago: University of Chicago Press.

Myers, Dowell. 1984. Turnover and Filtering of Post-war Single Family Homes. *Journal of the American Planning Association*. 50,3 (Summer) 352–358.

Myers, Phyllis. 1978. *Neighborhood Conservation and the Elderly*. Washington, D.C.: The Conservation Foundation.

Myers, Phyllis. 1982. *Aging in Place: Strategies to Help the Elderly Stay in Revitalizing Neighborhoods*. Washington, D.C.: The Conservation Foundation.

Myers, Phyllis, and Binder, Gordon. 1977. *Neighborhood Conservation: Lessons from 3 Cities*. Washington, D.C.: Conservation Foundation.

National Urban Coalition. 1974. *Urban Homesteading: Process and Potential*. Washington, D.C.

Niebanck, P.L., and Yessian, M. 1968. *Relocation in Urban Planning: From Obstacle to Opportunity*. Philadelphia: University of Pennsylvania Press.

Nourse, Hugh O. 1976. A Rationale for Government Intervention in Housing: The External Benefit of Good Housing, Particularly with Respect to Neighborhood Property Values. In *Housing in the Seventies*. U.S. Department of Housing and Urban Development. Washington, D.C.: U.S. Government Printing Office.

Onaka, J.L. 1983. A multiple attribute housing disequilibrium model of residential mobility. *Environment and Planning. A* 15, 751–765.

Orfield, Gary. 1981. *Toward a Strategy for Urban Integration: Lessons in School and Housing Policy from Twelve Cities*. New York: Ford Foundation.

Pedone, Carla. 1982. *The NHS Neighborhoods and Program Impacts*. Washington, D.C.: Urban Systems, Research and Engineering, Inc.

Pedone, Carla I.; Remch, Patricia M.; and Case, Karl E. 1980. *The Urban Homesteading Program: An Assessment of Its Impact on Demonstration Neighborhoods, 1977–1979*. Cambridge, Mass.: Urban Systems, Research and Engineering, Inc.

Public Affairs Counseling Inc. 1975. *Dynamics of Neighborhood Change*. Washington, D.C.: U.S. Department of Housing and Urban Development.

Quigley, John, and Weinberg, Daniel H. 1977. Residential mobility: A review and synthesis. *International Regional Science Review*. 2,1 (Fall): 41–66.

Raspberry, William. 1985. Problems of the Underclass. *Cincinnati Enquirer*. May 27, 1985.

Rose, Harold M. 1971. *The Black Ghetto: A Spatial Behavioral Perspective*. New York: McGraw Hill Company.

Rugo, Robert. 1979. *Living in Boston: An Innovative Project of Public*

172 NEIGHBORHOOD UPGRADING

Information and Promotional Strategies in Support of Neighborhood Preservation. Boston: City of Boston, Office of Program Development.

Sacco, John. 1984. Changing Strategies in Urban Revitalization: Impacts of the Community Development Block Grant. *Journal of Urban Affairs* 6,2: 179–187.

Schill, Michael H., and Nathan, Richard P. 1983. *Revitalizing America's Cities: Neighborhood Reinvestment and Displacement.* Albany, N.Y.: State University of New York Press.

Schnare, Ann B. 1979. *Household Mobility in Urban Homesteading Neighborhoods: Implications for Displacement.* Washington D.C.: U.S. Department of Housing and Urban Development.

Schoenberg, Sandra P., and Rosenbaum, Patricia C. 1980. *Neighborhoods that Work: Sources for Viability in the Inner City.* New Brunswick, N.J.: Rutgers University Press.

Segal, David. 1977. *Urban Economics.* Homewood, Illinois: Richard D. Irwin, Inc.

Shear, William B., and Carpenter, Bruce E. 1982. *Housing Rehabilitation, Move Decisions and Neighborhood Change: An Analysis with the Annual Housing Survey.* Germantown, Maryland: HUD USER.

Solomon, Arthur P., and Vandell, Kerry D. 1982. Alternative Perspectives on Neighborhood Decline. *Journal of the American Planning Association.* 48 (Winter): 81–92.

Speare, Alden Jr.; Goldstein, Sidney; and Frey, William H. 1974. *Residential Mobility, Migration and Metropolitan Change.* Cambridge, Mass.: Ballinger Publishing Company.

Sternlieb, George. 1966. *The Tenement Landlord.* New Brunswick: Rutgers University Press.

Struyk, R.J. 1976. *The Housing Situation of Elderly Americans.* Washington, D.C.: Urban Institute.

Taeuber, Karl, and Taeuber, Alma. 1965. *Negroes in Cities: Racial Segregation and Neighborhood Change.* Chicago: Aldine.

U.S. Department of Housing and Urban Development. 1979. *Neighborhoods: A Self Help Sampler.* Washington, D.C.: HUD.

———. 1981. *Residential Displacement—An Update, Report to Congress.* Washington, D.C.: HUD.

———. 1983. *Working Partners: 100 Success Stories of Local Community Development: Public Private Partnerships at Work.* Washington, D.C.: HUD.

———. 1984. *The President's National Urban Policy Report.* Washington, D.C.: HUD.

U.S. Department of Housing and Urban Development. Office of Program Planning and Evaluation, Region 4, Atlanta. 1979. *Urban Housing Resources. A Neighborhood Targeting Approach.* Atlanta: HUD.

U.S. Senate Committee on Banking, Housing and Urban Affairs. 1977. Statement before the Committee by Patricia Roberts Harris, Secretary of HUD, September 8, 1977.

Urban Systems, Research and Engineering, Inc. 1977a. *Evaluation of the Urban Homesteading Demonstration Program. First Annual Report.* Washington, D.C.: HUD.

———. 1977b. *The Urban Homesteading Catalog: Volumes 1, 2, 3.* Washington, D.C.: HUD.

———. 1978. *Evaluation of the Urban Homesteading Demonstration Program. Second Annual Report.* Washington D.C.: HUD.

———. 1979. *Evaluation of the Urban Homesteading Demonstration Program. Third Annual Report.* Washington, D.C.: HUD.

———. 1980. *Creating Local Partnerships: The Role of the Urban Reinvestment Task Force in Developing Neighborhood Housing Service Organizations.* Washington, D.C.: HUD.

———. 1983. *Evaluation of the Urban Homesteading Demonstration. Final Report. Volume 1: Summary Assessment.* Washington, D.C.: HUD.

Vandell, Kerry D. 1981. The Effects of Racial Composition on Neighborhood Succession. *Urban Studies.* 18: 315–333.

Varady, David P. 1971. The Household Migration Decision in Racially Changing Neighborhoods. Ph.D. diss., University of Pennsylvania.

———. 1979. *Ethnic Minorities in Urban Areas: A Case Study of Racially Changing Communities.* Boston: Martinus Nijhoff.

———. 1982a. Indirect Benefits of Subsidized Housing Programs. *Journal of the American Planning Association.* 48,4 (Autumn): 432–440.

————. 1982b. Neighborhood Stabilization in Jewish Communities: A Comparative Analysis. *Contemporary Jewry.* 6,1 (Spring/Summer): 18–35.

————.1983. Determinants of Residential Mobility Decisions: The Role of Government Services in Relation to Other Factors. *Journal of the American Planning Association.* 49,2 (Spring): 184–199.

————. 1984. Residential Mobility in the Urban Homesteading Demonstration Neighborhoods. *Journal of the American Planning Association.* 50,3 (Summer): 346–351.

————. Forthcoming. Neighborhood Racial Change: The Wynnefield Story. In Murray Friedman, ed., *Philadelphia Jewish Life: 1940 to 1985.* Philadelphia: Seth Press.

Varady, David P., and Torok, Liz. 1984. Neighborhood Revitalization and Socioeconomic Stabilization: Changes in Eight UHD Neighborhoods between 1970 and 1980. Paper presented at the Midcontinent Regional Science Association meeting, Chicago, Illinois, May 4, 1984.

Wilkes, Paul. 1971. As the Blacks Move In the Ethnics Move Out. *New York Times Magazine.* January 24, 1971.

Williams, Dennis, and Simons, Pamela Ellis. 1977. Integration: Success in Oak Park. *Newsweek.* October 17, 1977.

Wireman, Peggy. 1984. *Urban Neighborhoods, Networks and Families: New Forms for Old Values.* Lexington, Mass.: Lexington Books.

Woodstock Institute. 1982. *Evaluation of the Illinois Neighborhood Development Corporation.* Washington, D.C.: HUD.

Zais, James P., and Thibodeau, Thomas G. 1983. *The Elderly and Urban Housing.* Washington, D.C.: The Urban Institute Press.

Index

175